216

W9-APF-464

**Mary Guleserian and
Therese Furey**

Tyndale House Publishers, Wheaton, Illinois

THE ULTIMATE BABY-SITTER'S SURVIVAL GUIDE

Copyright © 1996 by Mary Guleserian and Therese Furey.
All rights reserved. International copyright secured.

Library of Congress Cataloging-in-Publication Data
Guleserian, Mary.
    The ultimate baby-sitter's survival guide / Mary Guleserian and Therese
Furey.
        p.   cm.
        ISBN 1-56179-665-4
        1. Baby-sitting—Handbooks, manuals, etc. I. Furey, Therese.
II. Title.
HQ769.5.G85   1996
649'.1'0248—dc20   96-22915
                                                                    CIP
                                                                    AC

A Focus on the Family book published by Tyndale House Publishers, Wheaton,
Illinois.

Most illustrations in this book were done by Shara Braithwaithe. The
illustrations on pages 96–99 and 107–109 were done by BC Studios.

Editor: Colorado Wordmaster
Cover Designer: Candi L. Park
Cover Illustration: Dennis Jones

Printed in the United States of America

99 00 01 02 03 04 05 / 12 11 10 9 8 7 6 5 4 3 2

To Michael, Joel, Josh, Gabe,
Bridget, and Sarah

Contents

Acknowledgments

I wish to acknowledge the invaluable assistance of the following people: Lloyd and Sylvia Cotton, for their motivating encouragement; Carol McAllister, for her powerful "fishing lesson"; Linda Paszkiewicz, for her cheerful way of keeping me accountable; Chloe Sellens, for her refreshing editing; Susan Mow, who gave me help as often as I needed it, no matter how many miles separated us, and who was a selfless mentor.

Deep respect and admiration go to my husband, Armen, who revived my spirit when he discerned the need, for his ceaseless patience, kindness, and love, and for allowing six weeks to turn into two years. I thank my wonderful sons, Joel and Joshua, for their energy, enthusiasm, and support.

Therese and I both wish to thank our mother for her faith in us, her support, guidance, wonderful suggestions, and above all the seven brothers and sisters we have to love and share.

Finally, we'd like to thank our father for bolstering our confidence and for his hearty laughs and unfailing support and encouragement—many thanks, Dad, for being there.

Mary

I wish to acknowledge the following people for their contributions: My dear husband, Joe—thank you for your continuous support, and most of all, for your character, humor, and filling our home with laughter. My children, Gabe, Sarah, and Bridget—your encouragement, excitement, and ideas were greatly appreciated.

My sister-in-law Kathi Duffy gave encouraging words and insightfulness with children.

My sister Mary, by her example, belief, and perseverance, ran the race to the finish. Thanks for the invite!

Therese

SPECIAL THANKS

To Barbie Love, a valuable friend and nurse who contributed in the first-aid section. Thank you so much for your willingness to educate us with your knowledge and for giving us your time and effort.

And to our editor, Michele Kendall, whose sweet spirit extends over the miles that separate us. Thanks for your hard work and patience.

A NOTE TO PARENTS

When parents go out for an evening these days, too often they hire a baby-sitter, put snacks on the kitchen counter, park everyone in front of the television—and walk out the door. While they're gone, children get to soak up three hours of sexual humor, outright adultery, murder, and mayhem on TV.

Enough! Let's change that.

What do we want for our children while we're gone? We want them in a safe atmosphere characterized by family principles such as cooperation, sharing, and caring.

This book prepares a baby-sitter for most problems that arise and gives alternatives to television: games that will challenge and inspire your children . . . simple, safe science experiments to open up whole new worlds . . . even a handy first-aid guide in case of emergency.

Your sitter—usually a young teen girl, but sometimes a boy—wants to do a good job. (If she doesn't, find a new sitter fast!) But a 12- or 13-year-old may not have all the needed imagination and knowledge. By providing this book to your baby-sitter, and perhaps even reviewing it with her, you can make sure your children receive a quality experience while you're gone.

Advice

THE FINE ART OF BABY-SITTING

Welcome to the world of taking good care of other people's kids and getting paid for it!

Of course, the job has its complex moments, which is why you need this survival guide. Here you'll learn how to deal with lines such as "My mom said I could stay up as long as I want" and "I can too have seconds on dessert!" You will learn how to handle an infant who just won't stop crying and fussing. You will also learn to better understand children and their feelings. The first-aid section will prepare you for emergencies that sometimes happen. We will teach you how to start your job right and then stay in control through the entire evening.

WHAT TO CHARGE

So you've decided to baby-sit to earn extra cash. You put your name up on the church bulletin board, and your mom has tactfully informed her friends that you're available. You think you're ready!

Sure enough, the phone rings, and Mrs. R. asks you to sit for her little four-year-old, Josh. You are excited until she says, "So, how much are you charging per hour?" Can you just blurt out what you want?

You hedge, "Ah, just a moment, please," cover the phone, and make faces at your parents. They're no help. You get back on the line and say, "Well, um, whatever you want to give me is fine." But you feel bad on the inside about that.

Don't sell yourself short! You are taking care of the most

valuable possession a parent has: children. There is absolutely nothing wrong with putting on your most positive, upbeat voice and answering, "Thanks for asking; my rate is ____ an hour." Say what you think is fair!

What's the worst that can happen? You lose the job. In that case, you can always make adjustments on the next phone call.

Things to consider before you quote a price:
- What are other baby-sitters in the neighborhood charging?
- How many kids will you be looking after?
- Are you expected to prepare meals?
- Are the parents going to be out past midnight?
- If so, charge a dollar more per hour after midnight.

Get the money question settled in the beginning; don't leave it to chance.

Some helpful points:
- If a second parent wants you to baby-sit his/her child as well at the first parent's home, this should not be a "free ride." You deserve an extra amount per hour beyond what you are charging the first parent.
- If being paid by check creates a hassle for you, then go ahead and say you prefer cash. This is entirely reasonable.

TURNING DOWN A JOB
You may run into some situations where you don't feel like working. It may be because you have a science project

or a history report to do, or you just want to spend time with your family or friends. We want you to know it's okay to say, "No thank you."

Sometimes it's hard to say no when you've just started to sit for a family. But if your reason is a sound one, go ahead. If the parent continues to pressure you after you've said no, stay firm, especially if you do not feel up to the task of child care. It's better to say no than to buckle under and resent the children.

If you ever encounter a situation in a home that makes you personally uncomfortable—for example, if something illegal or immoral seems to be going on—do not hesitate to tell your parents. They have insight into the appropriate behavior of adults and can be of great help to you.

YOUR ARRIVAL

The first time you sit for a family, tell the parent that you would like to come early to get to know the children before anyone leaves. Also, you'd like to familiarize yourself with the house and where things are kept. This shows your new employer that you're intelligent and want to do the right thing.

Have a paper and pencil handy when you ask the following 19 questions and TAKE NOTES. (Your employer will be impressed!) We recommend using 3x5 cards and creating a file on each household. Then bring the file along each time you baby-sit.

1. May I see around the house? Are any rooms off-limits to the children?

2. Are the children allowed to play outside?

3. Are there any medical conditions I need to be aware of, such as asthma or food allergies? Do I need to give any medications? (Write them down!)

4. Is there a first-aid kit? If not, where are the Band-Aids and antiseptic for "owies"? (You might even bring your own first-aid kit.)

5. What are the address and phone number of this home? *(Write them down! Many phones no longer have the number on them. If there was an emergency, you could go crazy trying to come up with the home's address and/or phone number in a hurry.)*

6. Where are the candles, matches, flashlight, and batteries kept, in case the electricity goes out?

7. Where is the circuit breaker box (main electrical switch)? Where is the main gas valve, and how does it turn off?

8. What is the plan for lunch or dinner? What, if any, snacks are allowed? (See page 26 under "Meals" for more information.)

9. How do I work the microwave and range?

10. When is naptime or bedtime?

11. Is there a phone number where I can reach you while you're gone? What about an additional beeper or cellular number?

12. Are there any animals I need to meet? Have they been fed? Are they allowed in the house?

13. What are the phone numbers of:
- the children's doctor
- the fire department
- the police department
- the poison control center
- a trustworthy neighbor or relative

14. Are you expecting any deliveries (pizza, UPS, etc.)? Any visitors? Repairmen?

15. Is there a gun in the house? Are the children aware of it? Is it locked away? Do the kids know where the key is? Would you mind putting it entirely out of range for this evening?

16. What TV programs, if any, are permissible? What time should the television be turned off?

17. Are the children allowed to use the computer (if the family has one)? For how long? What applications/games? Are there rules about going online?

18. Are all household cleaners, chemicals, and medicines kept in a locked cabinet? If not, how do I make sure they're out of reach?

19. Is any child not feeling well tonight? Do I need to give any medications? What are the exact doses? At what times should they be given? *(Write all information down! In fact, if a child has a temperature above 101 degrees F., vomiting, or diarrhea, these are good reasons to decline the baby-sitting job altogether. A child in that condition needs to be with his parent or other adult relative. It's also wise not to sit if you aren't feeling well. Be honest here; don't try to cover up. Tell the parent if you think you are coming down with something. Make sure you give plenty of notice. If you offer to find one of your responsible friends to fill in for you, be sure to give her/his qualifications.)*

PARENTS' DEPARTURE

As the adults are putting on their coats to leave, you might mention that if they find themselves running late at the end of the evening or wish to stay a little longer than they had planned, to please call you so you can let your parents know you'll be late.

Then turn your full attention to the children.

Can you remember being in a new environment where you didn't know anyone and you felt uncomfortable or nervous? Did you ever receive the gift of a smile? It is so easy to give and it brings instant reassurance. Children in your care are often frightened of somebody new, especially when they know their mom and/or dad is leaving. So do your best to bring warmth and comfort by smiling and encouraging the kids.

If the child is clinging to Mom and won't let go, your standing around and stalling isn't going to help matters. Firmly take the child in your arms, or by the hand, and say, "Bye-bye, Mom! Wave good-bye, Joel. We'll see you when you get back." This may unleash a mighty howl of

protest, but don't react. Close the front door, lock it, and walk immediately to a new attraction. Ask Joel to show you his room or his favorite toy. Start to play a game. Turn on some gentle music. The screaming will soon pass.

If you have been sitting for this family in the past, you've probably noticed that Gabriel's favorite snack is beef jerky and Bridget's favorite is bubble gum lollipops. This would be a wonderful time to bring the appropriate snacks out of your bag. You'll be a hero!

THE 10 "DON'TS" OF BABY-SITTING

Some things are out of bounds if you want to be known as a great baby-sitter:

1. DON'T have a friend "help" on your baby-sitting job unless the employer has given advance permission. It's easy for a friend to distract you from your job as a sitter. If the parent does agree to a friend coming over, ask somebody who is kind and likes and respects children.

2. DON'T play rough with the children. The less strenuous physical contact the better. Children may seem tough, but they can easily be hurt—and then you're in a major mess.

3. DON'T "substitute" for yourself. You may be tempted, for example, to have an older brother or sister take care of an infant while you finish a page of math homework. Don't do it! You are being paid to oversee all the children's activities. They are your responsibility!

4. DON'T tie up the phone. Again, you weren't hired to talk to your friends.

5. DON'T be a snoop, going through closets or

dresser drawers. Respect people's privacy.

6. DON'T allow outside people into the home unless you know them. Even if they say they are friends, neighbors, or relatives, apologize and say, "I'm sorry, but Mrs. D. didn't authorize me to let anyone in. Would you like to come back later or leave a phone number?"

7. DON'T use headphones. You need to hear everything that is going on in the house.

8. DON'T watch your favorite TV shows while the kids are awake. You may get engrossed in your program and miss what the children are doing.

The last two are super-obvious:

9. DON'T smoke on the job. We now know that secondhand smoke is dangerous to kids' health . . . not to mention the bad example you're setting for them.

10. DON'T touch anything alcoholic while watching children. You must remain alert. Any parents worth their salt would fire you if they found out.

INCOMING TELEPHONE CALLS

Don't volunteer that parents are not at home; simply say they are unavailable at this time. Write all messages down, including the time you took the call and the caller's name and phone number. Leave these messages in a safe and obvious place.

FEARSOME PETS

You're cleaning up after drawing all evening. You take the trash bag out to the side yard, throw it into the can, turn around—and face a snarling German shepherd!

STOP immediately. Don't move; don't turn your back to the dog. Most dogs will back off after growling and barking a bit. Don't run, but slowly take one step at a time.

Remember, this is his territory. Speak to him in a calm manner, and as you do, try to walk toward the door. If he doesn't back off, cross your arms across your chest, or put your hands in your pockets (to make it harder for him to bite those areas). Keep trying to get to the door. Don't look the dog directly in the eyes—he'll consider it a challenge.

This can be mighty scary, and hopefully the parent has clued you in to Rover's disposition. It's never fun having the wits scared out of you. That's why we included Question 12 in the big list a few pages back.

DISCIPLINE

You're probably thinking, *I'm too young to discipline any-body. That's the parents' job.*

Yes, it is. But a certain amount of control is necessary for you to do your baby-sitting job, which includes keeping kids as safe as possible. So, to put it simply: When you need to warn a child, say, "Stop and think!" Explain to the child what he is doing wrong. Teach him what is right—calmly.

If the kids are obedient, then you've lucked out. If they aren't, there is no way you can change them in one evening. But you can sit down with them and explain that you have three main rules while you're baby-sitting:

1. When I say no, I mean no!

2. If I ask you to do something, I expect your cooperation.

3. While I'm here, I'm in charge. Your parents have hired me to take care of you. If you disagree with something, you can discuss it with them when they get home.

State the three rules so you can show them you are in control and thereby hopefully avoid a power struggle. If a power struggle does happen, get down on their level, look into their eyes, and quietly say, "This seems to be a problem for you. Can you tell me about it?" In other words, let the children give their reasons. Kids need to know you care how they feel. But in the end, enforce what needs to be enforced.

Try, however, to focus on the positive. If the kids are being good and playing nicely, tell them how wonderful they are. If they are cooperating or participating, tell them you like their attitude. You can forestall a lot of fights this way.

Magic Word

Let's say you see Joel slug Josh on the arm, and when you correct him, Joel complains, "But Josh took my toy!" Or you asked Gabe to clear off the table, and he saunters into the TV room and says over his shoulder, "I never do the dishes." Or Sarah comes in complaining that "Bridget left her dirty clothes in the bathroom and won't pick them up."

You smile firmly and say, "NEVERTHELESS, Joel, we can't hit when we're angry."

"NEVERTHELESS, Gabe, I asked you to clear off the table." (You may also offer to help him if you think it's wise.)

"NEVERTHELESS, Bridget, I'm asking you to pick up your clothes."

When children are in the terrible twos and threes, it's easy to get locked into power struggles. About this age, the child learns that he has a will of his own. He will continue begging and whining as long as this behavior works.

Don't let this frustrate you. Just stick to explaining the rules and following through.

CONSEQUENCES
Kids don't like to be left out of the action, so when they misbehave, you need be firm about the consequences. Have them sit in a remote place for five minutes or less. Be matter-of-fact and keep your voice calm. Explain to the child what rule he broke, how he broke it, and that this period of inactivity is the consequence. Encourage the child by telling him you know this will help him learn to follow directions next time.

With an older child, the procedure is the same as above, only you can go up to 10 minutes—no more (even if you think he deserves 30 years!). Don't forget to use eye contact, speak gently, and let him know that although the behavior was wrong, you're quite sure he will do better in the future.

Other consequences that work include taking away a privilege, such as: no television, no Nintendo, no playing with a friend.

Follow through on the rules and consequences so the kids know you mean what you say. They will test you on this! If you follow through, your job will be much easier. They will then respect you in the other things you ask of them.

TAKING CARE OF BABIES

In addition to the earlier list of questions, ask the parents of an infant about the following:

1. What specific food do you want the baby to eat?

2. What is your baby's schedule? Does the baby eat every three hours or "on demand"? *(Some parents choose to feed the baby whenever she seems hungry.)*

3. Is the baby fed only formula, or is water or juice an option?

4. How many liquid ounces do you feed the baby?

5. How would you like me to heat the bottle? *(You probably already know how to test the temperature after heating. Sprinkle a little from the bottle onto the inside of your wrist. It should be lukewarm to warm, but not hot.)*

6. Do you lay the baby down to sleep on his tummy or back?

7. Does the baby go to sleep easily, or should I expect some fussing?

8. If the baby does fuss, would you like me to pick him up right away or let him cry? If so, for how long?

9. Besides milk, is the baby eating solid food or baby food? *(Always use a spoon instead of a fork to feed an infant, by the way.)*

10. Does the baby use a swing? A playpen? For how long in each case? *(Be careful not to bump the baby's head when placing her in or taking her out of a swing.)*

11. How does the side of the crib lower and raise? *(Be sure to keep the side up when the baby is sleeping.)*

12. Does the baby go to sleep with a pacifier? If so, where is it kept?

HCS

13. Is the baby teething? Is there a gel or a teether to help with the pain?

14. Is there a special blanket or stuffed animal the baby sleeps with?

These questions will really help you to know what to expect, so make sure you ask.

SPECIAL PROBLEMS WITH BABIES

In the first couple of months, infants usually sleep for the better part of the day, waking only to be fed or have their diapers changed. Remember, crying is their only way of communicating that they need something. Be gentle but persistent until you figure out just what it is they need.

If the baby is fussy, check for these things:

- Has the baby burped? There is always the possibility of trapped gas.
- Does the baby need to be changed? Urine can make the skin start to burn, which is painful.
- Remove the wet diaper, wipe the area, use what the parents have been using in terms of lotions or creams, and rediaper.
- Is the baby overdressed or underdressed for the weather?
- Is the baby hungry?
- Is the baby tired and ready for a nap?

To console a crying infant, wrap him securely in a blanket. Give him a pacifier (if he uses one) and walk him. Turn on soft music or the TV, and put the lights low. Move to a darker room if you have to.

Never hold a baby in a feeding position, because she will think she's going to eat.

THE COLICKY BABY

Unfortunately, colic occurs in some infants from the time they are born to about the end of the third month. These infants draw up their legs and scream as if they are in terrible pain. They are! They have either swallowed air because of feeding too fast or too slow or have drunk overheated milk. Sometimes colic is caused by an allergic reaction to the formula.

What to do:

- Try to stay calm.
- Make sure the baby isn't hungry.
- Burp the baby after each ounce.
- Let the baby use a pacifier.
- Try walking with the baby, talking softly and gently.
- Try placing the infant in a swing.
- If there is trapped gas, try placing the baby on his back, then grasp his ankles, and move the legs slowly in a pedaling motion. As you press them gently in toward his tummy, he may pass gas and find relief from the pain.
- If the baby won't stop crying, and you're really frustrated, call the parents.

NEWBORNS

Be very, very careful. Always remember to support the head and neck. Newborns have not yet developed the muscle strength to hold up their heads during the first couple of months of life.

If you are standing while holding a baby, be careful to watch where you are going. Don't turn quickly. Walk slowly; you don't want to bump the baby's head on a doorjamb as you walk from room to room.

Never leave an infant unattended on a bed or changing table. She can roll right off and get seriously hurt.

When awake, infants are taking in information all the time. They are really very smart! Babies love to be rocked, sung to, and spoken to gently. There is no reason why you can't read aloud to a baby who is awake.

ATTENTION! TAKE CARE!

Infants up to two years can scream piercing, deadly screams. Sometimes you can't console the child no matter what you try. Sometimes you are sure there is no reason for the screaming, such as a pin pricking him, or a dirty diaper. It can be a terribly upsetting experience for you. But you still have to remain calm. Count to 10 if you find yourself losing your patience.

NEVER shake an infant or a child. This can cause permanent brain damage and even death. You see, the baby's skull is bigger than his brain, so when a baby is shaken, his brain is slapped against the walls of his skull, resulting in severe and permanent damage.

If screaming persists, call the parents. If you cannot reach them, call a neighbor or other phone number the parents left with you. If you can't locate any help, call your own parents.

UP TO SIX MONTHS

Babies soon learn to lift their heads while lying on their stomachs. They also like to follow lights, mobiles, and moving objects. At about three months, babies become more alert and playful. Try holding out a toy in front of the baby, or putting him down on a blanket with a few of his toys. Slowly move one of his toys out in front of him and let him try to follow and grasp it. Again, give smiles and eye contact. You'll be rewarded with coos, smiles, and giggles.

Babies, however, cannot handle too much playtime at once. Limit it to a couple of minutes. Little ones can be overstimulated and get fussy. Once he starts looking away, stop.

As a baby approaches six months of age, she can sit up with some assistance. You might want to put a pillow behind her for support. Babies at this age like the game Peek-a-Boo. Hold up a pillow in front of your face, then pull it away, and with a big, happy smile say, "Peek-a-boo!"

For another game, try laying the baby on his back. You can start your fingers down at his toes and work your way up, crawling up his body to his chin, saying, "I'm going to kiss you!" and end with a kiss on the forehead.

SIX TO 12 MONTHS

Babies learn to crawl at this age, and you have to watch them every second. They don't understand the dangers of tablecloths and vases and glass-top coffee tables, so be on the alert!

One thing they can't hurt, however, is pots and pans. If you don't mind the noise, get out a couple of pans and turn them upside down. Hand the baby a wooden or metal spoon, and let the racket begin!

A CAUTIONARY NOTE: If you are holding a baby in your arms, sometimes he will lunge either forward to what he sees, or backward if he doesn't want to be held and wants to get down. So ALWAYS hold the baby with both your arms.

If you use a playpen, you'll see how some babies love to throw toys out of the pen. This is a game for them. Pick up the toys and put them back in. They'll do it over and over, as long as you're willing. They are learning that they can pick things up and drop them.

When sitting in a high chair, babies of this age learn they can release whatever they are holding. The fact that the gooey, sticky food will fall onto a clean floor is beside the point. No amount of yelling "OH NO!" will make sense to this child. The tone of your voice will tell him, however, that you're mad at him for . . . what? He has no idea. So save your scolding.

It's a good idea to put down newspapers to catch the food, and place the high chair on a hard surface or floor that's easy to wipe clean.

12 TO 18 MONTHS

Babies this age are full of curiosity and will rush headlong into anything. You must be constantly on the alert. Make sure to watch any objects the baby puts in his mouth. One of the ways babies learn is by tasting. They don't know the difference between a worm and a "gummy bear." Youngsters can choke on coins, buttons, small toys, and hard candy.

Keep all balloons away from children this small, especially popped ones that little kids can put into their mouths and choke on. If you use balloons to play games, be sure to pick up all the popped ones and throw them away. Keep thinking and watching all the time!

Most infants at this age start to walk with the help of someone holding their hands. They love to practice walking; it makes them excited to see what they're accomplishing. They also start to play with balls or other toys. But be aware that they sometimes throw whatever it is they've picked up, not realizing it may be headed straight for someone's face.

Babies love to be talked to and held. Try walking outside. Keep a hat or bonnet on the baby's head so she does not get burned by the sun. If you stay outside for some time, use a sunscreen made for babies, taking care to put some on her ears and nose. Be careful, though, not to get sunscreen in the baby's eyes.

Talk about the colors of flowers. Show him plants and grass or buzzing insects. This activity is stimulating for a child. Kids this age also love music, so try putting some on and dancing while holding him carefully. Let the baby feel the rhythm and have fun.

All babies love to play with balls and bubbles. Peek-a-Boo still works, too; try using a small blanket as the screen.

TAKING CARE OF TODDLERS

18 TO 24 MONTHS

At this age, toddlers are busy and full of curiosity. Most walk by now and are climbing. They are constant bundles of energy, getting into everything! They will climb onto, over, and into anything and don't realize the possibility of danger. You MUST follow them and keep them in full view. Set up boundaries with doors locked or chairs blocking certain areas. Always keep the bathroom door closed. Some parents invest in baby gates so you can limit the distance the baby will travel.

Toddlers don't tire easily, so you've got to be alert at all times.

TWO YEARS AND UP

Everything a one-year-old can do, triple it! Toddlers can run, jump, and climb.

One of their favorite games is chase. Be careful when you play this. If you chase the child, he will be looking back over his shoulder at you, and that could be dangerous. It's a better idea to let the child chase you.

Kids love to play ball at this age. Take turns kicking the ball, or sit with your legs apart and roll the ball back and forth. Building blocks are also fun to play with toddlers.

Other ideas for play include Playdoh, bubbles, and role-playing—for example, fireman, police officer, nurse, shopping at the mall, clerking behind a counter.

Children love stories, so read to them. Don't be surprised, when you're finished, if the kids ask you to read the same story again and possibly again. Don't get frustrated with this. Don't you like to hear a favorite song over and over? It's the same with kids. They love repetition and expectation.

You might surprise children by bringing a treasured book or game from your childhood to share.

You can make up great stories of your own, too. But be sure not to tell scary ones. You'll have a lot of explaining to do when the parents call and ask you just what story it was that you told.

POTTY TRAINING

When you're baby-sitting a toddler, ask the parents how they would like you to handle this.

Some parents give specific rewards for the child using the toilet; others give verbal praise. Also, how often should you take the child to try? And at naptime, does the child use a diaper or not?

TEMPER TANTRUMS

Tantrums can be loud outbursts or a quieter attack of whining. Most of the time you'll get screaming and crying when a toddler feels he is being wronged or he doesn't get what he wants.

These displays can sometimes be avoided by changing the circumstances. If the toddler wants a certain toy and his sister also wants it, pick up the toddler and take him into another room to distract him, or offer him a different toy. Or, if weather permits, take the child outside. Does the youngster have a special doll, teddy bear, or blanket you can get for him to help distract him?

If none of these techniques work, leave the child alone to calm down. Tell him quietly (this is the key), "I'll be in the other room coloring (or looking at a favorite book, or playing with toys), and when you're ready to come out and be pleasant, I'll be waiting." After he's calmed down and come out of his room, offer a hug and encouragement, because children don't always remember why they were upset.

PLAYING OUTDOORS

Ask the parents what they allow and don't allow. For example, if they have a swing set, are the children allowed to climb and jump off it? How high? Ask for specifics, because children sometimes test the boundaries when their parents are gone.

If it's really warm, water games are a blast: running through a sprinkler, playing with water guns, and so on.

Drawing on the sidewalk with chalk or a paintbrush and water is also great fun.

TAKING CARE OF OLDER CHILDREN

THREE AND UP

Children at this age love to play just about anything that mimics real life, such as storekeeper, librarian, school-teacher, or policeman. Use your imagination, and you can really have a lot of fun. Try setting up an area like a fort. Use sofa cushions, blankets, and chairs. Kids love creating areas where they can crawl, maneuver, and pretend.

If the child has blocks or Legos, you can construct all sorts of things, and it's a great time to hold a conversation. Ask the child questions while you play. Make sure to give positive feedback. If the child says, "Let's build a fire station," you can respond, "That's a great idea; firemen are very brave because they run into places that are on fire to save people."

If you are willing to play with the kids, they'll have lots of ideas and never-ending energy.

THE DISABLED CHILD

If you are asked to sit for a child who is physically or mentally impaired, get extensive instructions on how to care for him. You must be strong and trained if you are required to lift a youngster who is in a wheelchair or bedridden. Be sure you are able to take on an important job such as this. It takes a very, very special baby-sitter to take care of disabled children.

MEALS

Sometimes you'll be asked to cook a meal. It may have been prepared earlier, and all you have to do is serve it up. Most of the time the parents will expect you to eat with their children. But remember these cautions:

- To be on the safe side, keep the children a few feet from any burner or microwave. Let them participate by setting the table instead. Children really want to be helpful, but they move too fast to be allowed near the stove. Tell them that when they are older, they can learn how to cook.

- The handle of a cooking pot on the stove should be turned to the side or to the back of the burner. You don't want children to reach up and grab a hot handle or pull the pot over on themselves.

- Never open up a package of food unless invited to do so. Don't eat the parents out of house and home! People have food planned for different days of the week. Ask, "Is there something you don't want the children to eat?"

- Be sure to turn off the oven after you've removed the dinner. If a parent says, "Oh, just feed them something from the fridge, or rustle something up," make it simple, like a tuna sandwich or peanut butter and jelly.

- Ask what snacks are available, and under what conditions. If Gabe wants an ice cream cone, does he have to finish his macaroni and cheese first?

FOODS TO AVOID

Never leave a child alone while eating a meal or a snack. The reason? Children can choke on food.

Hot dogs are the number one choking food of small children. It is also easy to choke on steak or any meat that is difficult to chew. Either cut it into tiny pieces, or avoid it altogether. We recommend you ask the parents if there is something else you can serve.

Soups sometimes can get very hot and easily burn a child. Be sure the soup you serve a child is cool enough before she starts eating it.

Marshmallows, corn chips, popcorn, and hard candy can get stuck in the throat and cause choking. If the parent says it's okay to serve these snacks, be alert in case a child has difficulty swallowing.

Grapes are safer if cut in half. Yes, it's time-consuming, but better to be safe.

When making peanut butter sandwiches, go easy on the peanut butter. Too much can stick in the child's throat.

CLEANUP

The parents ordered pizza, and was it good! Paper plates and napkins were set out, and all you had to do was pour the soda or lemonade. After eating, the kids rushed out to the backyard to play, and because you swore you'd never take your eyes off them, you decided to clean up the kitchen mess later.

A few hours later, you've finally bathed the kids, and after two bedtime stories, they are all tucked in. You look

around and see the fort the kids built in the living room. Construction toys are everywhere, and a handful of dolls are strewn about. The bathroom is a mess, water is on the floor, and the tub is still half full of toys. The dining room table is covered by the paper art you had been teaching the kids. And don't forget about that mess in the kitchen.

Oh, no! It's nine o'clock, and your favorite program is on! You eye the living room couch, just picturing yourself cozy and content in front of that TV.

Well, the problem with this little scenario is that it happens all too often in homes across this country. Your problem is that you did

not get the help of your little friends. So, let's try this again. . . .

The parents ordered pizza, and was it good! Paper plates and napkins were set out, and all you had to do was pour the soda or lemonade. Just before the kids finished eating, you said, "Hey, kids, let's all put our paper plates in the trash, okay? Now, let's see. I wonder who is going to be the neatest?

"Thank you for asking to be excused! How did you know I like that? I see Sarah washing her hands; thank you for remembering, Sarah! Who would like to take out the trash? Thanks, Gabe, I really appreciate that. Before we go out and play, let's be sure this table is wiped off. We want it clean for our snack in a little while. Did you say you liked yellow canary tongues for a snack? Oh, you didn't? Who was that?"

For toys that are strewn about and forts that are made inside the house, you have a contest to see who can pick up the most in a minute, making sure the items are not just thrown into another room of the house. You tell the children that everything has its place, and toys should go back where they belong. You praise even the smallest effort; next time the effort will be greater.

Children love to please when they know that their efforts are acknowledged. All parents appreciate a picked-up home when they arrive back.

BATHTIME

Some parents will have their children already bathed and ready for bed when you arrive. We recommend that you ask to be excused from bathing children, because accidents happen. However, some parents will want you to handle this duty regardless. If so, ask if the job includes a shampoo.

Of course, you would NEVER leave very young children unattended during bathtime. However, older children who can bathe themselves will want privacy; be sure to ask the parents what they prefer. Three-year-olds probably won't care whether or not you're in the room, but a six-year-old might.

Check the water temperature before allowing the child into the tub. Place YOUR inside wrist or arm into the water to test it. Never mind how it feels to your hand, because the hand can tolerate much higher temperatures than the inside of your wrist or arm.

On this same note: The last water to travel through the faucet should be cold. This brings the temperature of the steel faucet down (in case children grab it, which is an easy way to get burned). Keep a firm grip on youngsters, using one hand to hold on to them and the other to soap them.

Shampooing hair runs the risk of soap getting in the eyes, and rinsing hair can be awkward. Carefully explain to the child that you are going to put soap on his head, and then after you're finished, you are going to rinse it off. Tell him in advance whether you're going to tilt his head back to rinse under the faucet, or whether you are going to rinse by pouring a cup of water over the head. Finally, tell him that after you shampoo and rinse, you'll put a dry towel on his face.

For girls with long hair, use a blow dryer so they don't go to bed with a wet head. Do this job in another room, not in the bathroom. Why? Electrical objects such as blow dryers and curling irons need to stay away from water, sinks, and bathtubs.

If a child hits the roof and starts screaming during bathtime, forget it. It's not worth the hassle and could be dangerous. Simply get a washcloth and clean up the little tyke as best you can. Most parents will understand.

If you have kids in the tub playing games, with toys and bubbles flying, just make sure they actually use the soap and get clean. Help them out of the tub, and make sure they get completely dry before putting on their pajamas. Don't forget to clean up the bath area, mop up sloshed water with a towel, and put bath toys away. Rinse the tub out, and make sure the faucet is turned off.

BATHING INFANTS

Most parents have a small tub made of plastic that fits inside a regular tub or even a kitchen sink. Place the baby firmly inside, and strap her in. NEVER leave the baby alone, even in this plastic tub. If the phone rings, let it ring. Nothing is as important as the care of this child. Make sure the water temperature is warm but not too warm. Soap each area carefully and rinse thoroughly.

If the home does not have a handy little tub, and you have been asked to bathe an infant, take a terry cloth towel about the size of a hand towel and place it over your arm. This ensures against a soapy, wriggly baby squirming out of your grasp.

Work over a sink. If you are right-handed, put the baby into your left arm and use your right to sponge her with soap and water. Make sure you use a nontearing shampoo, one that is mild and doesn't sting the eyes. Two drops of shampoo is enough.

Have a dry, clean towel handy to pat the baby dry. Be sure to wipe little crevices and ears, but don't attempt to clean ears with cotton swabs; let the parents do this. It is too easy to rupture a membrane.

BEDTIME

Okay, the kids have had their baths, they are in their jammies, and it's seven-thirty. The parents have asked you to put the little tykes down at eight o'clock. Now is the time to start winding down.

Explain to the children that their bedtime is in half an hour. Tell them that as soon as they brush their teeth, get a drink, and use the bathroom one more time, you will read to them. Make sure they don't hand you a book that is 400 pages long. Explain that when eight o'clock comes, it's time for sleep.

One thing you could do is bring some books you loved to read as a child. But as we said before, no scary ones! Parents do not appreciate nightmares at three in the morning.

When eight o'clock arrives, go ahead and ask the children if they say a prayer before going to sleep. If so, encourage them to do so tonight as always. If they don't have this tradition, it was still good for you to bring up the subject and show your friendliness toward it.

You are responsible to the parents for getting the kids to bed on time. Children need rest, and no one knows better than the parent how much rest a child needs.

If you find the child testing your authority, and you've already given her a second glass of water and she's made two trips to the bathroom, you need to be firm. It's time for your magic word: No matter what her requests are, calmly say, "NEVERTHELESS, it's time for bed. Good night!" Then leave the room—no more discussion.

If they say they're scared, tell them that you'll pray with them, but after that, they will still stay in bed. You might leave a soft light on in the room. You may need to use your magic words more than once. Go ahead. It's a great response to the million times they'll ask, "Why?"

COLLECTING YOUR PAY

If, at the end of an evening, the parents say they cannot pay you, politely but clearly ask when the following day it would be convenient for you to come back and pick up your money.

If you keep having problems with these parents, calmly tell them the next time they call that you've decided not to continue sitting for them. They may ask you why, or they may not. If they do, say, "Getting paid at the end of the evening has seemed to be a problem, and so I think I'd rather decline the work." Yes, it's hard to be honest, but they need to learn.

The same thing applies to employers who cut you short for "lack of change." They owe you, say, 15 dollars . . . but they seem to have only a 20-dollar bill or a 10-dollar bill, so 10 dollars will have to do, "sorry about that." This is unfair and should be addressed. Politely remind them that when they hired you, they agreed to a certain rate. Then ask them when the following day it would be convenient for you to come back and pick up the full amount they owe you.

Games

INDOOR GAMES AND ACTIVITIES

Games are a great way to get to know the children in your care. You talk, laugh, and share good times that wouldn't happen if you just watched TV.

You can start by asking the kids for their favorites, such as board games. This shows them you have an interest in their preference. The evening can get crazy with loud games like Yahtzee, or intense with Jenga, or calm with the Ungame.

Other activities are not games per se, but are just as much fun: simply coloring together in a coloring book, for example.

Here is a wide assortment of things you can do with your children to use the time profitably:

GIVE A BLESSING

When you know the parents are going out for a special

 anniversary or birthday evening, sit down with the children and help them make cards with their own pictures and words. Use colored pencils, markers, crayons, and stickers; let the children have fun and be creative.

SHARING FAMILY PICTURES

Another way to get to know the children you are baby-sitting is to let them show you their family photo albums. *(Ask the parents to get them out for you before they leave.)* Even a child as young as 18 months can point to pictures of himself, Mom, Dad, sisters, brothers, pets, and so on. Kids take great pride in showing others their family.

TALENT NIGHT

Ask a child if he plays a musical instrument or has another talent to share, such as singing a song, reciting a poem or Bible verse, or reading a book out loud. And what about you? Do you have a talent you would like to share? Little children will be some of your most enthusiastic fans.

STOMPIN' HENRY

Materials Needed:
Balloons
String

Tie an inflated balloon on the leg of each child. At a signal, the kids try to stomp on and burst the other players' balloons. When a balloon bursts, that person is out of the game.

Some kids will not like it when their balloons are popped. You may get sudden tears, so explain BEFORE you start that you have plenty of balloons, but some are going to be popped, and that's part of the game. Be cheerful, and don't give in to wailing.

With this game, have the kids barefoot or in socks, and use a room that is kid-proof. You don't want them knocking over lamps or stepping on the cat's tail.

Throw away any balloons that have popped or are just lying around. Don't give little ones a chance to put these things into their mouths.

VICTORIOUS VOLLEYBALL

Materials Needed:
1 "net" *(Actually, it can be nothing more than yarn, string, a sheet, etc.)*
Balloons

Make a "net" between two chairs. The kids can either stand or sit as they bat the balloon back and forth across the "net." Again, we caution you to choose carefully where you play this game. Throw away all used balloons!

TURTLE RACE—*Ask parents' permission to use apples from the refrigerator before trying this one.*

Materials Needed:
Apples

Each child balances an apple on top of his head and walks to the goal line. If the apple falls off, the child must go back and begin again. When the race is finished, the players get to eat their apples!

COLD RUSH—*Ask parents' permission before trying this one.*

Materials Needed:
Spoons
String
Ice cream *(Yum!)*

Arrange teams of two, mixing younger and older kids as evenly as possible. Tie two spoons together with string,

leaving approximately six inches between them. Prepare two bowls of ice cream with the same amount of ice cream in each bowl. Then, on your mark, get set, GO! The teams wolf down their bowls of ice cream. Winners finish their ice cream first.

Don't bother looking up a remedy for a cold-rush headache in the first-aid guide. We checked, and there isn't one.

PRETZEL TOSS

Materials Needed:
Rolled socks or
ball of yarn

Have kids lie down and pitch a wadded pair of socks or a ball of yarn over their heads toward a target area, using only their feet.

For an even greater challenge, have them lie facedown and shoot for the target.

STATUE WRAP—*Ask parents' permission for this one.*

Materials Needed:
Toilet paper

Give two kids a roll of toilet paper, and have one creatively wrap the other into a statue.

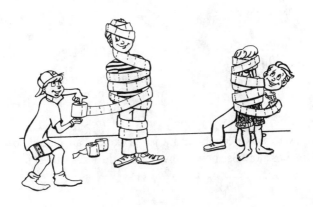

MIRROR WRITING

Materials Needed:
Blank paper
Crayons

For kids who know how to write, this is a lot of fun. On blank paper, children try to write a note to their mom or dad BACKWARDS. They may require several tries in order to succeed.

Then watch the fun as they give the note to their parents, who will need to hold it up to a mirror in order to read it.

HOOP DE LOOP (or BOGUS BASKETBALL)

Materials Needed:
Wire hanger
Balloons

Bend a wire hanger so a balloon can fit through it. Then hang it on a door. Stand three to four feet away, and try to make baskets.

OH, YOU NUT!

Materials Needed:
Peanuts
Can or jar

Try to toss peanuts into a jar or coffee can placed six inches away. See how many peanuts the kids can get into the can.

Then move the can progressively farther away.

GUM ART—*Ask parents' permission before trying this one.*

Materials Needed:
Poster board
Chewing gum

Give each child a piece of poster board or a thick card. Then hand out sticks of gum, and tell them to chew the gum until it is soft. Have them form some kind of art on the board or card with the chewed gum—for example, a flower, an animal, or perhaps a snake.

They'll probably want to do several pictures, so bring plenty of gum with you.

P.S. Little ones may not want to give up their gum. Be patient and let them see how the older kids do it, or you can demonstrate.

BEAUTY TIME
If you happen to have long hair, let young girls brush, braid, and put clips in it. They love to learn how to do different braids and hairstyles.

Another fun thing to do is to let the girls put makeup on you and on themselves. You must get permission from Mom for this unless you're using play makeup. Dressing up with costume jewelry is time-consuming and lots of fun for little girls.

MAKING MASKS

Materials Needed:
Heavy paper
(*like construction paper*)
Yarn or kite string
Scissors
Masking tape
Crayons, colored
pencils, or felt-tip pens

Making masks is a fun way to keep youngsters busy for hours. Sketch an animal, clown, or pirate (as shown). Let them color in the mask. This is a great time for encouragement and listening to little children.

Then let them carefully cut out the whole mask. Blunted scissors are best. When they cut out the eye holes, tell them to make sure they cut the holes large enough so they can see well through them.

Cut out the side holes, used to tie the mask. Reinforce the holes with masking tape. Bring string through the holes and tape down or tie a knot.

PAPER BAG PUPPETS

Materials Needed:
Paper lunch sacks
(any color)
Glue
Colored construction paper
Toothpicks
Colored marking pens
Cotton balls

You can really use your imagination with this craft, doing any animal or character.

For the rabbit puppet, sketch out the figure onto construction paper, then cut it out. Use different colors to create your masterpiece. After cutting out the head, glue it onto the bottom fold of the bag. For whiskers, use white construction paper, or you can use toothpicks.

The "Groucho" puppet is easily made by using black construction paper to make the eyebrows and mustache. Use a black felt pen to do the eyes, nose, and "suit."

WINDMILL FLOWERS

Materials Needed:
Square paper
(not a rectangle)
Tape
(masking or Scotch)
Paper clips
Green construction paper

Unfold your paper clip and follow the directions. You can use different colors of paper to make yourself a bouquet. For leaves, cut out a leaf and tape it to the paper clip.

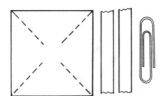

1. Supplies needed: square paper, tape, and paper clip.

3. Bring every other edge up and pierce it with the paper clip.

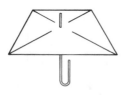

2. Pierce unfolded paper clip through center of paper.

4. Tape top and bottom of the windmill, to keep it in place.

DANCING WITH SCARVES

Give each child a scarf and put on some nice music. Show the kids how to twirl and make their scarves appear to float in the air.

SPONGE BALL BOWLING

Materials Needed:
Empty soda can or plastic bottle
Rubber or sponge-type ball

Sit 10 feet from another player who's near an empty soda can or plastic bottle. You then toss a rubber or sponge-type ball, trying to knock the bottle or can over. Each knockdown gets a point. Ten points wins the game.

LAUNDRY BASKET PULL

Materials Needed:
Plastic laundry basket
Blankets
Stuffed toys

This is great for indoors on a rainy day, especially with young children between the ages of one and a half and three.

Put blankets in a laundry basket along with the child's favorite stuffed animal. Next, you add the child! Pull the basket around the house, being careful to avoid areas near stairs. Kids love being zipped around in their "car." Be sure you put everything away when you're done.

SPAGHETTI BAGETTI

No, it's not time to eat, just time to play! With parents' permission, cook some spaghetti noodles about seven minutes in boiling water. *(Make sure you keep the kids out of the kitchen while you're boiling the water.)*

Drain the water and let the noodles cool for a few minutes. Then have fun using the spaghetti to "draw" on a paper or ceramic plate. Help write the child's name or practice the ABCs. It's up to you. Be creative!

MAKE YOUR OWN PLAY DOUGH—*Ask parents' permission for this one.*

Materials Needed:
6 tablespoons of oil
3 cups of flour
1 1/2 cups of salt
3 teaspoons of cream of tartar
A few drops of food coloring
3 cups of water

Mix all ingredients in a bowl. Then encourage kids to create or copy things they see. Be sure to cover their efforts with praise and compliments.

When you're finished, cleanup is a must. Put play dough in zipper-type baggies or an air-tight container. It will last for months.

This can be hours of fun and a great time to talk to the kids and get to know them.

RAINBOW RICE—*Ask parents' permission first.*

> **Materials Needed:**
> Rice, not cooked
> Zipper-type baggies
> Food coloring
> White glue
> Paper

This is a messy but fun project for kids four and older.

Put about a half a cup of rice into four different baggies. Add 10 drops of the same food coloring per bag. Then seal and shake so that the rice gets colored.

Now with your rainbow of colors, you can put glue on the paper, place the rice on top, and make a masterpiece.

THINKING GAMES

ENCYCLOPEDIA PUSH

This is a great way to spend time on a rainy afternoon and while away the hours. Seat the children next to you on the sofa and pick out the "F" encyclopedia. Flip to the page with all the flags of the nations, and then say to the children, "I'm looking at the flag of Switzerland." Have them try to find the flag, with you guiding them.

With older children, you can time the attempts at finding the flags the fastest. Other categories to consider are Trees, Birds, Dogs, Fish, and Flowers. This stimulates interest and teaches at the same time.

CALLING GAME

Form groups of two. Then call out, "Stand toe to toe! . . . Elbow to elbow! . . . Nose to nose!" etc., and let the kids follow directions.

Very young children love this game. It's also great for listening skills.

OLLIE, OLLIE, OPPOSITE

Call out a word such as "aerodynamic," and have kids quickly say the opposite. (Just kidding.)

Use words like "fat," and have the kids say the opposite. (It's "skinny" or "thin," in case you didn't know.) You might want to make a list ahead of time in order to keep the game moving along. Examples: no-yes, stop-go, happy-sad, salt-pepper, tall-short, fast-slow.

I PACK MY BAG

This is for kids who know their ABC's and like to be challenged. You start off by saying, "I'm packing my bag for Australia (or any place you prefer), and I put in apples."

Next, the child says, "I'm packing my bag for Australia, and I put in apples and books." The next player says, "I'm packing my bag for Australia, and I put in apples and books and cats." Each child adds an extra item, going in alphabetical order. The first one to skip a letter is out.

Once you get good at this, try limiting your game to foods or animals. An even more complicated version involves advancing the place-names along the alphabet simultaneously: Alaska, Botswana, Colombia. . . .

TELL ME A STORY

Have a small ball handy, any kind, or a ball of yarn, or a wadded up pair of clean (please) socks. You start a story, then hand the ball to the child, who must add on to keep the story going.

Example: "Josh could not believe it. There was a gorilla behind the cage talking to him! The gorilla seemed to be trying to tell him something. Every time Josh moved to walk away, the gorilla pleaded with him, his big hands outstretched toward him.

"'Hey, Josh,' said his father, 'that big guy seems to be talking to you.'

"'Maybe he's hungry and thinks you'll feed him,' said his mother.

"But Josh knew exactly what was going on."

At this point, pass the ball along to the next child to continue.

HOW'S THAT AGAIN?

Each child starts by sharing his most exciting adventure. For the first half of the game, have the kids tell actual experiences. Then during the second half, have them make up experiences using their imaginations.

Some kids won't get the hang of this at first, but be patient. Prod a little, and above all listen. This game is great for teaching kids to use their imaginations.

TIC-TAC-TOE

Yes, the old favorite. Kids love this so much they'll play it about a hundred times in a row. It takes two to play, and since kids love to be the "X" mark, go ahead and let them. You're the older, wiser one, right?

If you get bored with this one, try the one below.

WHO'S SQUARE?

Fill a page of lined paper with a grid of dots. Each person takes a turn connecting any two dots with a straight line. Diagonals are not permitted. The player who finishes a square puts her initial inside, and gets to take another turn immediately. When all the squares are captured, the player with the most squares wins.

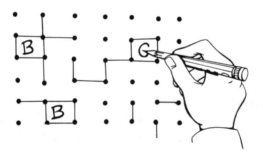

I SPY, I SPY

One player leaves the room. You tell the remaining kids to pick an item in the room. *(It has to be reasonably visible— not the gold thread running through the green curtains.)* Little ones will choose simple items, while older kids will get more creative.

When the person comes back into the room, everyone chants, "I spy, I spy something with my little eye, something that begins with 'C'!" Then the guesser gets to guess what begins with "C."

HICKORY HEIGHTS

This is for very young children. Shut your eyes, and have the child say, "I am very tall" or "I am very small." Then guess whether he is standing or sitting.

Even if you know the answer, guess the opposite so the child will think he is fooling you. Kids love fooling others.

UNITED ART

Give each child a piece of paper and a pencil. Tell the kids to fold the paper in half, then in half again. Without unfolding the paper, have everyone draw a head and a neck on the top quarter section of the paper.

When all are finished, each person passes the paper to the next child. *(If you are baby-sitting just one child, then you take it.)* The next task is to add a torso on the next quarter section of paper. *(Arms would be nice, too.)* The third addition, of course, is the legs down to the knees.

Finally, everyone adds a pair of lower legs and feet.

Don't let anyone see what is being drawn until the very end. Then unfold the papers and proudly display your united efforts on the fridge!

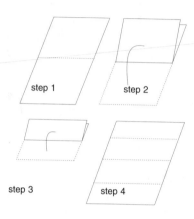

step 1

step 2

step 3

step 4

ART CLASS

Get out crayons and paper, then just sit, relax, and draw with the children. They'll love having you sit with them. Maybe play some music while giving them ideas for drawings, if needed, or help if they ask. Be sure to praise their efforts and their final work.

OUTDOOR GAMES AND ACTIVITIES

WACKY-WET-WONDERFUL

Materials Needed:
Water-filled balloons

Two kids (or you and one kid) stand facing each other, starting at arm's length apart. Toss a water balloon underhand, gently, from one to the other. After each throw, the players take a step back. This goes on, with the players getting farther and farther apart, until the balloon bursts.

SOFT-DRINK RELAY

Materials Needed:
Empty plastic
soda bottles

Teams should consist of three or more kids. Fill a soft-drink plastic liter bottle full of water for each team. Form two lines.

The first runners must shove their thumbs into the tops of the bottles, turn them upside down, and run to a goal line and back. The bottles must stay upside down,

although they will lose water. The winners are judged on how much water was saved.

This is great fun, especially if you can get enough kids from the neighborhood to play.

FILL-'ER-UP RELAY

Materials Needed:
4 plastic pitchers
2 plastic cups

Form two teams. Each team has one empty pitcher and one full pitcher of water. The empty pitcher is on the starting line, while the full pitcher is at the goal line.

At your signal, the first kids in line race to the full pitcher, fill a plastic cup with water, and race back to dump it into their team's empty pitcher. As soon as the runner is done, the next takes off with the empty cup. First team to fill their pitcher wins.

PICKLE!

Set up two bases approximately 10 yards apart. Then have two players, each with a foot on a base, toss a SOFT ball back and forth. A third player runs back and forth between the bases, trying not to get tagged by a player holding the ball.

In order for the game to progress, each runner attempts to tag the opposite base five times. If the runner cannot make a base without risk of getting tagged by his fifth attempt, he is automatically out. *(This five-try limit is so the runner doesn't just hang out between bases.)* Once a player gets tagged, it is someone else's turn.

DRESS-UP RELAY

We've included this game because it is so much fun and a great icebreaker. We've used it at birthday parties and even showers for adults! It's also great for classrooms on rainy days or even sunny days. If you're baby-sitting only two or

three kids, recruit some from the neighborhood if you can. Have the kids form two lines. At the goal line, place all the materials into two separate piles, one "outfit" for each team.

Call for everyone's attention and proceed to demonstrate what will happen. Each and every single player must put on a hat, both socks, and one pair of gloves with fingers in all the way. Then the player removes them, runs back to the starting point, and tags the next player, who does the same. The team to finish first wins.

SAFE SCIENCE EXPERIMENTS

SAFETY PRECAUTIONS

The activities in this section are safe with the appropriate supervision. As the world's best baby-sitter, you already know that you never leave children alone. Some of these experiments require help from an older person; others can be carried out by the children themselves, if they are old enough. But you should always be watching and attentive.

Remember to encourage children to ask questions. Listen to their answers, and help them explore new possibilities. Praise them for their efforts.

Also, follow these guidelines:

1. Clean surfaces before and after you try experiments.
2. Follow directions step by step.
3. No rough or rowdy behavior allowed!
4. Clean up spills immediately.

STRAW, POTATO, PUSH!—*Ask parents' permission for this one (unless you bring your own potatoes and straws).*

Materials Needed:
Raw potato
Plastic straws

This is such a mindblower for little ones. Toss the potato in your hand; feel the weight of it. Have the kids do the same. Then say, "Think I can push this straw through this potato?"

1. Put the potato on the table or kitchen counter and hold it firmly with one hand, making sure the palm of your hand is not underneath.

2. With a fast, strong push, stab the potato with the straw.

3. What happened? Did the straw bend? The straw should go into the potato. If it didn't, try again with another, or try faster and harder. You may surprise yourself and push it clear through.

Why? An object remains at rest (the potato, in this case) or keeps moving (the straw, in this case) unless it is acted upon by some external force (your brute strength).

TWO-STRAW TRICK

Materials Needed:
2 straws
1 glass of water, juice, or milk
Determination

Put one straw in the glass. Keep the other straw outside the glass. Put both straws in your mouth. Now drink from the straws. Hey! What happened? You only sucked up air!

Try again! What? It happened again! Why do you suppose you did not get any liquid?

What you need to do is place your tongue over the top of the straw that is outside the glass. This will allow you to quench your thirst—and amaze your kids!

CHALLENGE!

Materials Needed:
Paper
1 glass
1 clear container *(plastic or glass)*

Tell the children that air takes up space. Tell them to fan themselves and ask if they can feel that.

Now tell them that you can put paper inside water and it won't get wet! Crumple the paper and place it tightly into the bottom of the glass. Fill your plastic or glass container half full of water. Turn the glass upside down, and put it into the container, taking care to keep the glass straight (vertical) as you push down.

The paper doesn't get wet! Ask the children why. Listen to their answers. Even if what they say doesn't make sense, you can reinforce them with comments such as "Wow, you're really trying to figure this out—that's great!"

When you're ready to explain the trick, ask the children, "What's in this glass? Paper, right! Anything else? Well, sometimes nothing is something. Guess what? Air is in the glass and holding the water back. Air takes up space! When I pushed the glass full of air and paper into the water, the air inside kept the water out of the glass. Air has a lot of power, doesn't it?"

Let the children try it. Let them try taking the paper out and letting the air escape. The bubbles and the gluppy burps of water are especially fun for kids.

SHHH ... LET'S LISTEN

Materials Needed:
Pencils *(on paper)*
Jars with screw-top lids
Keys, coins,
paperbacks
(for flipping pages),
wrinkled foil wrap, plastic wrap,
kitchen utensils, or whatever you
find handy that will make unusual
sounds so kids can discover the
art of listening

Tell the children that this is a quiet game: No talking unless it is your turn to guess. Caution the others who are waiting their turns not to say anything even if they think they know the answer.

Have the children close their eyes. Then pick up an object and make noise with it. Ask one child to name what he thinks he is hearing. Help him describe it. If it's foil being scrunched, say, "This is a scrunchy sound." Or if you wave a flat piece of foil, tell them to notice the various pitches in sound. Are the sounds soft? Loud? Sharp? Tinny?

LIGHT BENDS!

Materials Needed:
Jar of water
Piece of paper
Pen or pencil

Draw a happy face without the smile on a piece of paper. Place the paper on the table. Place the jar of water on the paper in front of the happy-face figure. Looking THROUGH the jar, take your pencil and try to draw a smile on your happy face. As you learn to adjust, try drawing a body, arms, and legs on your figure. Why is it difficult?

The shape of the jar is round. There is more water at the center of the jar than at the sides. Light rays coming into the jar are bending, and the water acts as a magnifying glass.

Try placing things like coins, paper clips, or tiny toys inside the jar, and put identical coins, paper clips, and toys outside the jar. Compare the difference.

WHERE IS IT?

Materials Needed:
1 clear glass
(Be sure the base isn't too thick.)
1 penny
1 saucer
(plastic or ceramic, not glass)

This is a great little science lesson about how the light reflected from an object reaches your eyes.

Fill the glass with water all the way to the top. Place the water glass on top of the coin. Now cover the top of the glass with the saucer. Challenge the children: "Can you see the penny? Look through the glass! Look at the bottom! Where is it?"

Lift the glass to assure the children that it's not a trick; the coin is there. But the light needed to reflect to your eyes is being blocked by the saucer. The light rays are bent as they pass from the glass, and bent again going through water. The saucer prevents you from seeing the coin.

Now remove the saucer and look straight down. Do you see it? For another optical illusion, remove the saucer and look at the top of the water from the side. The coin will appear to be on the surface.

DISAPPEARING ACT

Materials Needed:
Shallow pan or
glass jar
Marking pen or
grease pencil

Fill a shallow pan or glass jar with water, and tell the children that you are going to study evaporation. Have them say the word a couple of times. Good job!

Tell them that water disappears or is absorbed into the air, and this disappearing act is called evaporation. Mark the jar when you start, and then several hours later see if the level has gone down.

It's best to do this on a warm day. Explain how the sun vaporizes the water into the air and makes air very moist in some parts of our country. That's called humidity.

Do a simpler version for very young ones. Try wetting the ground and letting them walk barefoot through a puddle, then walk to a dry area and make crazy footprints. It doesn't take long to watch the wet footprints dry out.

GO FLOAT!

Materials Needed:
Shallow pan of water
Many different objects
of various weights
*(Go through the kids' toys and pick
objects that will sink or float.)*

Do this one on the kitchen table or near the kitchen sink. Place a couple of paper towels on the counter nearby.

Mark one towel "Floaters" and one "Sinkers."

Spread the objects out and have the children guess, "Will it float or will it sink?" Have them try their objects and explain why each one behaves the way it does. Remember to be supportive of the children's guesses. "Good job! Way to think! Well, let's try it!"

Talk to the children, asking why some things float. "What kind of material is this block made of? Why do you think a wooden block sinks and a plastic block floats? Are all things that float alike? Are they different? How are they alike?"

TOUCHY, TOUCHY!

Materials Needed:
Gather together all types of objects of
different sizes, shapes, textures:
things like tape, sandpaper,
cotton terry cloth, rocks, graham
crackers, stuffed toys, sponges,
erasers,
dice, etc.
(Use your imagination!)
Large paper bag

Place everything on a large table, and let the kids look at the objects. Then have them close their eyes while you place an object in the bag. Let each child, in turn, touch the object and say how it feels. Is it soft? Bumpy? Rough? Sticky? Let him guess what it is; then have him pull it out. Reward with positive feedback and praise.

HOW MANY PENNIES?

Materials Needed:
1 glass
1 dry cloth
10 pennies

Rub the top edge of the glass with a dry cloth. Pour water into the glass until it is full, or even slightly above the top. Now have one child carefully drop a penny edgewise into the water. Slowly drop more pennies.

Ask, "Will one more penny cause the water to flow over?" Have the kids keep taking turns dropping pennies in. Who will be the one to make it overflow? Remember to have them look at the surface tension of the water. It seems to be over the rim of the glass!

BOING-BOING!

Materials Needed:
Square or rectangular aluminum cake pan
Assorted rubber bands

Have children examine the rubber bands. What makes them different? Some are thick, and some are thin; some are long, and some are short.

Place different rubber bands around the cake pan. Pluck them and watch them vibrate. Ask the children, "Does the vibration have anything to do with the sound? Which bands make loud or soft sounds? Does the length or width of the band have anything to do with it?" *(Yes. Where they are placed on the pan also makes a difference.)*

Sound is caused by vibration. Thick produces a low sound and vibrates slowly. Thin produces a high sound and vibrates quickly.

WANNA BET?

Materials Needed:
Glass of water
Several cardboard squares that
will fit over the opening of the
glass

Bring the children to the kitchen sink or outdoors. *(This one can get messy.)* Fill the glass with water, then dump it out. Tell the kids you will now turn the glass over without spilling the water. They'll naturally wonder how.

Fill the glass three-quarters full and place the cardboard over the top. Turn the glass over quickly, remove your hand from the cardboard, and air will hold the cardboard in place as the water remains in the glass . . . for a short time. When the cardboard absorbs the water, it will fall off. *(And we have had the wet kitchen floor to prove it.)*

Explain that when the glass is turned upside down, a partial vacuum is formed in the glass. As air tries to fill the vacuum, the air pressure put on the cardboard holds it in place. Let each child give it a whirl.

LOOP-DE-LOU, WHOOP-DE-DO, MOBIUS STRIPS

Materials Needed:
Construction paper
(any color)
Tape and scissors
Pencil or pen

Set A—Cut four strips of paper 11 inches long and a half inch wide. Tape the ends of one strip to form an untwisted loop. Using scissors, cut the loop along the center line. Now you have two loops.

Set B—Take a second strip. Twist one end and tape the ends together. This is a single-twist loop. Cut the single twisted loop along the center line as in the first set. Hey! What happened? Instead of two separate loops as before, you end up with one longer loop.

Set C—Take a third strip, and give one end two twists. Tape the ends together. This is a double-twist loop. Now cut the loop along the center line. What do you have? The loop with two twists becomes two loops that pass through each other. This is called a Möbius strip.

Set D—Take a strip, give one end a half twist, and tape it to the other end. Get a pencil and draw a line down the middle. It will be continuous. You'll never cross the edge. A twisted loop has no inside or outside. It has only one side.

MUD PIES—*Ask parents' permission first.*

Materials Needed:
Hose
Water
Dirt
Spoons
Jar lids

Add about a tablespoon of dirt and a teaspoon of water to a jar lid or dish. Have the kids mix it up. Let them dry-bake in the sun. If the weather is overcast and damp, you can use the oven (again, get permission).

Do the pies hold the shape you originally wanted? If they come apart, they're not sticky enough. Try digging down deeper to get more claylike dirt.

As mud dries, it shrinks. No doubt you will have cracking. You can prevent this by adding straw to mud. The straw soaks up the water and keeps it from collecting in spots. The mud now dries evenly.

Ask, "If you took a leaf and made an impression on the mud pie, would it stay?" Try it! "How about a dead bug?"

OVERFLOW

Materials Needed:
Glass of water
Paper towels
Eyedropper or straw

Place the glass on top of a paper towel. Fill it to the top with water. Challenge, "How many drops can you add to the glass before it overflows and runs down the sides?"

Have the kids get eye level with the top of the glass. What can they see? Take turns adding water with the dropper. Try not to be the one who makes it overflow.

Tell them the bulge of water at the top of the glass is held together by the water's surface tension.

DON'T SINK THE RAFT!

Materials Needed:
Large pan or bucket filled with water
5-inch square of aluminum foil
100 paper clips

Ask, "If I place this sheet of foil on the top of the water and then place a paper clip on it, will it sink? How many paper clips do you think our raft will hold?" Have the kids guess and write down their numbers, along with their names. Make it fun and exciting!

When the raft sinks, dry it off and try again. Say things like, "You know, if I space the clips out more evenly, I wonder if it will hold more." *(Make sure that if a baby is watching, he doesn't put clips into his mouth.)*

MIRROR, MIRROR

Materials Needed:
Mirror
Paper
Pencil with eraser

Prop a mirror in front of two books or any object that will support it at a desk or kitchen table.

At the top of the paper, draw a squiggly line. Now fold the sheet so that you can't see the line you've drawn, only its reflection in the mirror. Challenge the children to copy the line while looking only in the mirror!

Explain that what they see in the mirror is the reverse of what you've drawn on the paper. If you want to turn left with your pencil, your brain tells you to turn the opposite way.

Try this again with letters or figures of cats, dogs, or trees.

TOWER OF STRENGTH

Materials Needed:
Construction paper
Various sizes of books
Rubber bands or tape

Ask, "Can you think of a way to put a book on top of a sheet of construction paper so it will stay?"

Hold the construction paper vertically. Place a book on top; of course, it falls flat. Fold the construction paper into a V shape, placing the book on top. It falls flat again.

Now roll the paper into a tube, and secure it with a rubber band or tape to keep it from unrolling. Place the book on top. TA-DA!

Ask, "Why do you suppose it held?" Well, the tube shape made the paper strong enough to support the book. Let children experiment. Praise their efforts!

EGGS-R-EASY —*Ask parents' permission first.*

Materials Needed:
Several hard-boiled eggs
Several raw eggs—same size
and color
1 ceramic or plastic plate

Gently mingle the hard-boiled and raw eggs together on the table. Then say, "Okay, which ones are raw, and which are cooked?" Tell them you're going to show which is which.

Place an egg on the plate, narrow end up, and spin it like a top. If it is hard-boiled, it will continue to rotate because its center of gravity is in the thickest half. As it spins, it will stay upright.

The raw egg white prevents the uncooked egg from spinning, since the yolk is heavier. When you spin the egg, you'll get a clumsy rocking movement because of centrifugal force.

MUSICAL GLASSES

Materials Needed:
Glass of thin material, or a crystal glass
(Get permission if you use the crystal, and BE CAREFUL!)

Fill the glass with water. To remove all natural oils from your hands, wash with soap and dry them. Dip your index finger into the water, and rub it along the rim of the glass. It will vibrate, producing a wonderful ringing note.

You can change the tone by adding or removing water. Line up several glasses and form a musical team. Point out the vibrations on the surface of the water.

HOW DO YOU SPELL THAT?

Materials Needed:
3x5 cards
Pen or pencil

Find out if kids are right-handed or left-handed! Give

them a pen or pencil and a 3x5 card. Ask them to hold the card to their foreheads. Now tell them to write their names on the card.

They'll be surprised at what they write. It's rather like mirror writing. They really have to concentrate on what they're doing, starting

from right to left.

MAGNIFY THE MAGNIFICENT

Materials Needed:
Magnifying glass
*(You'll probably have
to bring this with you,
since many families
don't own one.)*

Tell the children that a magnifying glass helps us see things we don't even know are there. It also helps us see how objects are similar to or different from each other.

Use your magnifying glass to see:
- What's hidden in grass or under leaves
- What's on both sides of leaves

- How mosquitoes bite *(Ouch!)*
- Different patterns of snowflakes
- Butterfly wings, bugs, and other crawly critters
- Objects in the soil

If the children are old enough, have them draw pictures of what they see. Remember to encourage the little ones; they'll ask questions, and you can ask questions of them. Be sure to listen to their explanations. This helps them gain confidence in their thinking.

GIMME SOME SPACE

Materials Needed:
Kitchen sink
1 clear glass
1 flexible drinking straw

No two things can occupy the same space at the same time, as we all know from seeing two kids try to occupy the same chair.

But to prove this scientific fact, fill the sink half full with water. Fill the clear glass with water, and immerse it in the sink. Turn it upside down so the bottom of the glass is sticking out of the water.

Take the straw and bend it under the water into the glass that is upside down. Then blow air into the glass. The air will rise to the bottom of the glass (the part that is sticking out of the water). Air displaces the water into the sink. Now air occupies the bottom of the glass!

This shows that no two objects—no matter what shape, weight, or mass—can occupy the same space.

EASY DIFFUSION

Materials Needed:
1 clear glass
Food coloring
Eye dropper

Fill the glass half full of water. Let the kids choose a color. With the eye dropper, take some of the food coloring and put it in the bottom of the glass.

Explain that everything, including the water we drink and the air we breathe, is composed of tiny molecules. Tell the children that molecules move from an area of greater concentration to one of lesser concentration until they reach equilibrium. The coloring, although concentrated in the bottom of the glass at first, will gradually diffuse (spread outward).

What do the children observe? How long do they think it is going to take?

KNEE JERK

Materials Needed:
Willing child
Wooden spoon or rubber spatula

Have the child sit in a chair or on a countertop, with legs dangling. Tap GENTLY just below the knee with the spoon or spatula. The leg below the knee will jerk out. Explain that this shows how the information travels along the nerve-cell pathway from the tendon in the knee to the spinal cord and back to the muscles.

Kids love this and will want to try it on you or each other. That's fine; just don't allow them to forget the word *gently* during the tapping part.

SAY WHAT?

Have the child sit in a chair and ask him to close his eyes. No peeking!

Tell him you are going to snap your fingers around the chair, and he must point to the direction of the sound. He cannot move his head. He must sit straight up and be on the alert.

Sound perception is done by the ears. So if you stay in an area that is along the middle of the body and snap your fingers, he'll have trouble figuring out what direction it came from. Snap your fingers over, above, behind the ear. Try at the top of the head. Where is he having trouble?

Try hitting two toothpicks together. How different is that? How much more will he need to concentrate? Take turns trying different ways to trick one another.

SOAP POWER

Materials Needed:
Index cards
Scissors
Baking dish
(or a sink full of water)
Dishwashing liquid

From an index card, cut out a boat (see page 80). Make it about 2 1/2 inches long and 1 1/2 inches wide.

Place the boat gently on the water in the dish. Next, pour a little detergent into the notch in the end of the boat. What happens?

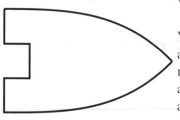

Your boat should zip across the water. Water molecules are strongly attracted to each other and stick close together, especially on the surface. This creates a strong but flexible "skin" on the water's surface that we call surface tension. Adding soap disrupts the arrangement of the water molecules and breaks the skin, making the boat go forward.

If you repeat the experiment, wash out the baking dish carefully each time, or your little boat won't go.

EC-STATIC!

Materials Needed:
Cool, dry day
2 round balloons
(inflated and tied)
2 20-inch pieces
of string
1 wool or acrylic sock

First tell the kids that all materials contain millions of tiny particles, called protons and electrons, that have electric charges. Protons have positive charges, and electrons have negative ones. Usually, they balance each other, but sometimes when two surfaces rub together, some of the electrons rub off one surface onto the other, and we have static electricity!

Then follow these steps:

1. Tie a string to each inflated balloon.

2. Rub a balloon on a child's hair for about 15 seconds. Be sure to rub around the whole balloon. What happens to the hair? What happens when you bring the balloon back close to the hair?

3. Let the kids rub the balloon on your hair.

4. Hold the string to each balloon, letting the balloons hang freely, but without letting them touch anything.

5. Slowly move the two balloons toward each other, but don't let them touch. What do you see? Do the balloons push away from each other, or do they pull toward each other?

6. Place your hand between the two hanging balloons. What happens?

7. Place a sock over one hand, and rub one balloon with the sock. Then let the balloon hang freely. Bring your sock-covered hand near the balloon. What happens?

8. Try rubbing both balloons with the sock, and then let them hang near each other. What happens?

9. Look for other examples of static electricity around the house. For example, have you ever felt a shock when you touched a metal doorknob on a cold winter day? What often happens when you remove clothes from the dryer?

BUBBLE PUFF

Materials Needed:
8 tablespoons dishwashing liquid
1 quart water
Drinking straws
Shallow tray

What to do:

1. Mix the dishwashing liquid with the water. Fill the shallow tray.

2. Ask the children to blow through their straws as they move slowly across the surface of the solution. How big are the bubbles they get?

3. Try making a very big bubble that covers the surface of the tray. Dip one end of the straw into the sudsy solution, then hold the straw slightly above the surface of the solution. Blow into it gently. The kids may have to try a couple of times to make a really big bubble. When they make a giant bubble, have them touch it with their fingers—first with a wet finger, then with a dry one. What happens?

4. Look closely at the bubbles that are being made. How many colors can the children see? Do the colors change?

BIG AND LITTLE CRITTERS

Materials Needed:
Insect guide and spider guide
from the bookstore or library
(preferably ones with pictures)
or an encyclopedia
Magnifying glass
No fear and a strong stomach
(Yikes!)

Search your home and neighborhood for bugs. **BE CAREFUL! PAY CLOSE ATTENTION!**

1. Look around your front yard and in cracks in the sidewalk. Look on lamps, on lights hanging from the center of the room (especially on warm, humid evenings), on plants, in crevices, in drawers (scary thought . . .), and in corners of rooms.

2. Identify types of bugs by using the guides. Depending on which part of the country you live in, you can have very different bugs. What have the children found? Ants? Spiders? Fleas? Silverfish? Moths? Flies? Ladybugs?

3. Ants can teach us how some insects work together as a community. Watch ants scurry in and out of their anthills. Watch them find spilled food on the sidewalk. Do they eat their food on the spot, or carry it back to their anthills?

4. When an ant finds food, it runs back to the hill to "tell" the others. As it runs, it leaves a trail that other ants can smell. The ants find the food by smelling their way along the trail.

5. Find out the difference between an insect and a spider. Why do spiders spin webs? What are webs made of?

Bugs do what they do to survive. They are constantly looking for food. Some bugs are both good and bad. Termites, for example, have a nasty reputation because they destroy people's houses by eating the wood. But they also break down dead trees, keeping the forest floor from becoming too cluttered.

CELERY SOAK

Materials Needed:
4 same-size stalks of fresh
celery with leaves
4 clear glasses
Red and blue food
coloring
Measuring cup
4 paper towels
Vegetable peeler
Ruler
Old newspaper

If you're baby-sitting all day on a Saturday or on a sum-
mer morning, start the day with this so you can observe
the results all day long.

1. Lay the four pieces of celery in a row on a cutting
board or counter so that the joints between the stalks
and the leaves match up.

2. Cut all four stalks of celery four inches below the
joint.

3. Put the four stalks in four separate cups of purple
water. *(Use 10 drops of red and 10 drops of blue food
coloring for each half cup of water.)*

4. Label four paper towels in the following way: "2
hours," "4 hours," "6 hours," and "8 hours." *(You may
need newspapers under the towels.)*

5. Every two hours from the time you put the celery
into the cups, remove one stalk and put it onto the
correct towel. *(Notice how long it takes for the leaves to
start to change.)*

6. Each time you remove a stalk from the water, with
the vegetable peeler carefully peel the end that was in
the water to see how far up the stalk the purple water
has traveled.

7. Ask the children what they observe. Did they notice how fast the water climbs the celery? Does this change as time goes by? In what way?

8. With your ruler, measure the distance the water has traveled.

9. What other things can you test for capillary action? Try paper towels, sponges, brown paper bags. How about flowers?

Explain that capillary action happens when water molecules are more attracted to the surface they travel along than to each other. In paper towels, the molecules move along tiny fibers in the towel. In plants, they move through narrow tubes that are actually called capillaries. Have the kids say it a couple of times. Plants couldn't survive without capillaries because they use the water to make their food.

MEASURING THINGS

Materials Needed:
Measuring spoons, measuring cups, containers of different sizes
(pint, quart, half-gallon, and gallon)
2 containers that hold the same amount but are different shapes
1 funnel
Bathtub or sink filled with water

First, we recommend doing this at the kitchen sink. If you ever do this at bathtime, have all the measuring things you need right there on the floor so you don't have to get up and go get something else. NEVER leave a child unattended in the bath. If the water is even a couple of inches deep, it's dangerous to children.

Tell your little charges that water and other liquids take the shape of whatever container they are in. Containers of certain sizes have names—for example, cup, pint, quart, or gallon.

1. Fill a small container (such as a quart) with water. Then pour the water (using the funnel) into a larger container (a half-gallon or larger).

2. How many tablespoons does it take to make half a cup? And how many cups make a quart?

3. Find out how many quarts it takes to fill a gallon.

4. Fill the gallon container, and use the funnel to pour the water into the little containers. How many times will it fill the pint container?

5. Fill a short container with a given amount of water—three cups, for example. Now pour this water into a tall container. Do your eyes try to tell you the tall, thin container holds more than the short, squat one? Does it hold more?

Be encouraging as you listen to the children's answers. Give them lots of praise.

Trouble

FIRST AID

NOTE: *Several of the first-aid techniques described in this section, such as CPR and the Heimlich maneuver, require technical proficiency in order to perform them safely. It would be wise for you to get formal training in first aid and, specifically, in the performance of these techniques. This section is not intended as medical advice nor as a substitute for formal training.*

Well, it's bound to happen sooner or later. You're in one room reading to the three-year-old when the six-year-old comes in screaming from the backyard, where he was building a fort. There is a nasty gash on his right knee, and blood is dripping down like a work of modern art. But lucky you, you've read this section of the book and therefore can calmly and quickly take care of the problem.

In this section, we'll cover everything from animal bites to vomiting. *(Yeah, it happens.)* Remember, when you arrived you asked for a quick tour of the house and to see where the first-aid kit is kept. Now you are ready to tackle any emergency.

ADVISORY: The 911 telephone number for emergency help doesn't work in every major city in the nation at this time. If you do not have 911, call your local fire department or police department and ask what the number is for emergencies. Write it down, and keep it with you during all baby-sitting jobs.

Also, to be prepared for medical emergencies, we recommend that you get *formal* CPR and first-aid training.

Okay, here we go—the Trouble Index, in alphabetical order!

BITES (BIG AND LITTLE CRITTERS)

ANIMAL BITES
Flush the wound with cool water and clean with mild soap. Cover with a clean towel. It is important to keep the child calm.

Try having the child describe what happened. What bit the child? Notify police if the animal is unknown—anything from a stray dog or cat to a wild coyote. Call the parents.

(Speaking of strange dogs, please refer to pages 6 and 10–11. This deals with your being prepared with facts about the family dog.)

INSECT STINGS
Symptoms include pain, swelling at the site, redness, itching and/or burning, headache, or muscle cramps.

Be aware that an allergic reaction to a sting can be life-threatening. Some symptoms are swelling of the eyes, lips, or tongue; coughing or wheezing; severe itching; stomach cramps, nausea, or vomiting; anxiety; difficulty in breathing; and dizziness. If any of these symptoms occur, call 911 and the parents immediately!

DO NOT pull the stinger out with tweezers, as this can squeeze more venom into the wound. Instead, scrape it out with your fingernail. Wash the area with soap and water.

Snake Bites

Call 911 immediately. Call the parents.

Keep the child quiet. Keep the bitten area (such as arm or leg) lower than the child's heart. Tell him that he is doing great and you are proud of him!

Tie a constricting band two to four inches above the bite, toward the body. Don't tie it so tightly, though, that it cuts off circulation. Wash the bite area with soap and water. Do not move the arm or leg of the bitten area. Keep the child calm. He'll be calm if you are calm.

Spider Bites

These can be dangerous. However, there are only three poisonous spiders in the continental United States: the brown recluse (or violin), the black widow, and the tarantula. In these cases, apply ice immediately and call the parents. If you can locate the spider that bit the child, bring it with you for identification.

BROKEN BONES

Is it really broken? If it is, the area around the site will be swollen, bruised, and possibly distorted. It will be painful, and any attempt to move that part of the body will cause a lot of noise to come from the child. Call Mom or Dad, because it's difficult to determine whether something is indeed broken or just severely sprained. Whichever, an X-ray will be needed.

There's going to be a lot of crying and shrieking. Keep your little patient calm, and speak soothingly. If you can't reach the child's parents, call your own parents or an emergency phone number that was left with you.

BRUISES

Cover with a cold wet cloth for 10 minutes while giving hugs and encouragement. You could start a game of grading bruises: "Wow, that's an 8 on a scale from 1 to 10!"

BURNS

Sarah lifts the lid on the stove to check out what's for lunch. She drops the lid and starts screaming from a nasty steam burn.

Take a deep breath and let your body calm down as you assess the situation; then approach the child calmly. Your blood pressure may be high, but don't let the child know you're excited or scared.

Please remember that any burn a child receives is going to cause terrible screams and crying. You'd cry, too! Tell her that you know it hurts badly and that you will help. DO NOT tell the child it's "not that bad" and to stop crying.

Is it serious enough to call the parents? Is it serious enough to call the doctor? The rule of thumb for most pediatricians is: if the burn is on the hands, face, trunk, feet, or genitals and is larger than a quarter, they want to be notified.

There are different kinds of burns:
- **First-degree** burns involve reddening and pain, but no blisters. Run cold water over the burn site.
- **Second-degree** burns involve redness, pain, swelling, and blisters. Run cold water over the burn for five to 10 minutes. If the area is large, get clean towels, dip them in cold water, and place them over the child. Repeat this process as the towels lose their coolness.

NEVER use ointment, oil, or butter on a burn. NEVER pop blisters or use fluffy dressings, like a cotton ball.

If arms or legs are burned, elevate them above the child's heart level, using a pillow. Call for medical help. Check for shock—the skin may be cold and clammy; the pulse may be fast and weak. The child's face may be pale, and he may complain of dizziness or nausea. Speech can be slurred; restlessness and anxiety may be apparent.

- **Third-degree** burns involve injury to all layers of skin, showing a white or charred appearance, with little pain. Obviously, call 911 or the appropriate emergency number for your area.

DO NOT try to remove burned clothing, bedding, or anything foreign to the body from the burned area. DO NOT put ice on the burn, because it may injure the skin layers.

CHOKING

Gabriel tells a joke at the table, and everybody starts laughing except Josh. The hot dog he was eating got stuck. He begins to panic and grabs his throat.

WHAT TO DO:
- **If** the child is coughing or is able to talk, stand by only! He'll get it resolved before long.
- **If NO SOUND** (or a high-pitched whine) comes from the child, turn to the "OBSTRUCTED AIRWAY" sections of this book (pages 106–110)!

CONVULSIONS

Yes, convulsions can be frightening. A child's eyes may roll upward, and his lips may turn blue. Breathing may stop. There may be loss of bladder and/or bowel control, or foaming at the mouth.

WHAT TO DO:
1. Do not try to stop or restrain the child in any way.

2. Protect the child by removing furniture, toys, or anything he may hit accidentally.

3. Loosen any tight clothing around the throat or waist.

4. When the seizure is over, check to see if the child is breathing normally. Reassure the child and talk quietly.

5. Call 911 IMMEDIATELY; then contact the parents.

CPR (Cardiopulmonary Resuscitation)

NOTE: *CPR is an important life-saving technique. Although this section describes the technique, it is not intended as a substitute for formal training. You should obtain formal first-aid training that includes the performance of CPR.*

Cardiopulmonary resuscitation is a technique used in emergencies when someone is not breathing and has no heartbeat. As you go through the following steps, think "ABC" carefully. "ABC" means Airway, Breathing, and Circulation.

Airway

Breathing

Circulation

CPR FOR INFANTS (up to 12 months old)

1. Check unresponsiveness: Tap or gently shake the baby's shoulder to see if he responds.

2. Call out for help if the baby doesn't respond.

Airway
3. Lay the baby on a hard surface. Gently tilt the head back ... not too far.

Breathing

4. Look for the chest rising. Put your ear to the baby's mouth to listen for breathing. Feel for the breath on your ear. If nothing's happening, cover the baby's mouth and nose with your mouth, making a tight seal. Give two puffs of air into the nose and mouth with only enough force to make the chest rise. If the chest does not rise, something is blocking the airway. (See pages 106–108 for what to do if an infant has an obstructed airway.) Lift the baby's chin slightly, and try two more puffs.

Circulation

5. Check for a heartbeat (pulse): Press your index and middle finger slightly above the bend of the baby's arm inside the elbow. Hold your fingers there for five to 10 seconds. DO NOT use your thumb to take the pulse!

6. If there is no pulse, place two fingertips (index and middle) on the baby's breastbone. Imagine a line drawn across the baby's chest between the nipples. Place your fingertips one finger width below that line. Press down to a depth of 1/2 inch to 1 inch. Do five compressions for every breath. In other words, press five times quickly, then give a rescue breath; press five more times, then give another breath.

7. After 20 cycles, check again for a pulse and breathing. If there is no heartbeat and no breathing, give two breaths and CALL 911 (unless help is already on the way).

CPR FOR CHILDREN (ages one to eight)

1. Check unresponsiveness by gently shaking the child's shoulder. Shout, "Are you okay?"
2. Call out for help if the child doesn't respond.

Airway
3. Position the child on his back, supporting the head and neck as you do so.
4. Open the airway by placing one hand on his forehead and the other hand's forefingers on his jaw. Tilt the child's head back.

Breathing
5. Put your ear over the mouth, while focusing on the child's chest.

- **LOOK**—Is the chest rising?
- **LISTEN**—Is air moving in and out?
- **FEEL**—Do you feel breath against your ear?

6. If the answers are yes, that's good news. If the answers are no, proceed with rescue breathing.

Pinch the child's nose with your fingers; place your mouth over the child's, and give two quick breaths.

7. If you don't get the results you want, check for an obstructed airway (see pages 108–110). If you get partial results, give two more quick rescue breaths.

Circulation

8. Tilt the head upward with one hand. With your other hand, find the Adam's apple in the center of

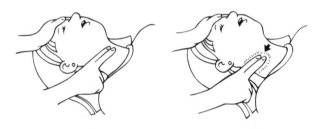

the child's neck, under the chin. Then spread your index and middle fingers each to a side in order to check the carotid pulse. DO NOT use your thumb to take a pulse! Never press on the Adam's apple—you can block the airway.

9. If no pulse is present, CALL 911. While you're waiting:

10. Find the lowest point of the breastbone. Place the palm of your other hand above your fingers, as in the diagram. Press down 1 to 1 1/2 inches at a rate of 80–100 times a minute.

11. After five compressions, stop to give one rescue (mouth-to-mouth) breath. Keep doing this cycle (five compressions, one rescue breath) for 20 cycles. Check pulse and breathing every few minutes.

THE RECOVERY POSITION (see diagram)

A breathing, unconscious child should be placed in this position while waiting for help to arrive. He is placed on his side so he can breathe easily. Sometimes children who have almost drowned or who have concussions will feel nauseated and may vomit. The recovery position keeps them from aspirating (inhaling) vomit.

Be sure to keep the top leg bent. The top arm also should be bent, and the top of the hand placed under the cheek.

CUTS AND SCRAPES

Slight bleeding from a cut or a painful scrape will usually stop on its own in a couple of minutes. However, you should give lots of sympathy. In situations like this, kids want their mom or dad. Tell them how brave they are and how proud you are of them. Some kids act as if they've been impaled, while others act as though it's nothing. Judge each situation on its own.

WHEN TO CALL THE PARENTS:

If the cut is deep, or if the shape of the cut is jagged, or if the cut is on the child's face and the edges can't be held by a Band-Aid, call the parents.

WHEN TO CALL 911:

If blood gushes or spurts from a wound, or if you've applied pressure for several minutes and it still doesn't stop, call 911.

DROWNING

Of course, you would NEVER, EVER, EVER leave a child alone in a bathtub, in the kitchen sink (if you are bathing an infant there), or in a small outdoor plastic pool. NOTHING can be important enough to leave him alone—not a phone call, not the doorbell (we don't care if you're expecting the president of the whole world). You know it doesn't take but the blink of an eye for a child to slip beneath the water, and it doesn't take a lot of water either.

Children lack coordination and thinking skills to protect themselves from drowning even in a few inches of water. Young children do not resist or struggle in the water. They will swallow water, sink, and lose consciousness in less than a minute.

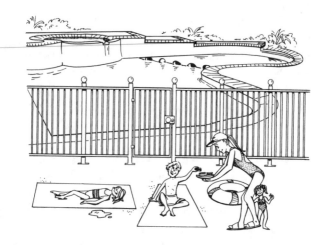

Children under three are especially vulnerable to drowning. So be protective of your curious, aggressive kids who are unaware of potential danger. Parents are often surprised to discover that their children can climb out of cribs, open doors, and go into areas that parents normally think are inaccessible. Be very watchful!

WHAT TO DO:
- *Call 911.*
- *Begin CPR at once.*
- *Pray.*

Just between us—even if the kids are old enough to swim, have taken lessons, and the parents tell you, "Oh, you can let them swim; just keep an eye on them"—we don't recommend the practice unless the children are at least nine and are expert swimmers.

However, if the kids insist and really want to swim, review the following rules:

1. No roughhousing. Perhaps you could set up and encourage relays to keep your charges busy.

2. No running. Then watch and make sure!

3. If you go in swimming with them, make sure you are not distracted at one end while two-and-a-half-year-old Josh is left with floaties in the shallow end.

4. Make sure you know CPR.

5. NEVER leave the pool area for any reason. If you have to go to the bathroom or answer the phone, have everyone get out of the pool and go outside the fence. Bundle them up in warm towels, or have them lie flat in the sun while you run into the house. Then get back immediately. Better yet, take them in the house with you. No phone call or doorbell is worth losing a child.

ELECTRIC SHOCK
Call 911 immediately.

Also:

1. Switch off the current if at all possible. You must be wearing rubber-soled shoes or shoes that will not conduct electricity. If the child is still trapped by a wire or whatever caused the shock, try to knock the object away with a wooden object, such as a broom handle or a wooden chair.

2. Check breathing and heartbeat at once. If they're not apparent, start mouth-to-mouth resuscitation immediately.

3. If the child is breathing, place her in a recovery position (see diagram on page 99) and get medical help immediately. Comfort and reassure the child to relieve her anxiety.

EYE
If something foreign gets into the child's eye, DO NOT LET THE CHILD RUB IT! This is going to sound impossible, especially if the child is yelling bloody murder. But remember this: If there are hot tears, they may flush the foreign object out.

WHAT TO DO:

1. Tell the child that you need to see inside her eye. Speak in soft, calm tones, reassuring the child as you go. Place the child in a good light and try to have her look up as you pull down the lower lid. Speak as you are doing this, informing

the child what is taking place. If you do see the object, try to remove it with a clean cloth or a tissue.

2. If you see nothing, tell the child, "Hmm . . . nothing here." Then pull the upper lid out over the lower lid and let it slide back. This may help to dislodge the object, even though you can't see it.

3. If you see the object, tell the child. Hopefully, she will remain still enough for you to get it out. If you get it out, great! But if you don't, then cover the eye with a soft pad and call the parents.

FALLS

All kids who are healthy and active will fall down. There's usually a lot of crying and fussing, so don't hesitate to give an equal amount of sympathy and attention to the "owie."

But if a child slips off a swing set or some other high place, you could be looking at something more serious.

WHEN TO CALL 911:
- **If** there is clear fluid.
- **If** there's an indentation in the skull.
- **If** there's bleeding from the ears.
- **If** the child is vomiting.
- **If** the child appears stunned.
- **If** the child is unconscious.

In all of these cases, DO NOT allow the child to rise up or move. Do not move the neck. If a child falls two feet or more headfirst onto concrete, call 911 and the parents. Keep the child's neck and back firmly supported.

FEVER

Occasionally, parents will leave you with a child with a "slight" temperature. Hopefully, they're nice enough to inform you of this! In such cases, follow the directions the parents give you concerning medication. There will probably be acetaminophen (Tylenol) in the medicine cabinet. *(Never give aspirin, since it may be dangerous to children.)* Usually parents will also ask you to give the child something to drink, such as cool water, to make him more comfortable.

But what about the times when the parents have left, and within an hour or two, the child is raging hot? You do not have to take the child's temperature to know he has a fever.

WHAT TO DO:

1. Notify the parents immediately, taking note of these details:

- **Is** there a rash with the fever?
- **Is** the child crying and pulling at an ear?
- **Is** the child breathing rapidly?
- **Does** the child have diarrhea?
- **Is** there a runny nose?
- **Is** the child perhaps just dressed too warmly for the hot weather?
- **Are** there complaints of abdominal pain or a sore throat? Is the child vomiting?

2. Remove constricting clothing from the child, and put on a light T-shirt. Do not cover the child with a blanket.

3. Sponge the child's forehead with a cool, wet cloth. Then wipe his neck, chest, and arms.

4. You'll get a lot of complaints and crying. A child may say he is too cold and wants a blanket. Assure him that he will feel better if you continue to sponge him with a cool cloth.

FEVER CONVULSIONS

Convulsions can occur when children have a sudden high elevation in temperature. They are VERY frightening. However, these convulsions do not mean something is terribly wrong; they just mean the body is dealing with the sudden fever in the only way it knows how—by shaking.

WHAT YOU'LL OBSERVE:

The child stiffens while clenching fists and teeth. The eyes will roll back, and the child will hold his breath. He may turn a little blue. Sometimes the child will stiffen or jerk suddenly, then completely relax like a rag doll. The arms and legs may dangle listlessly.

WHAT TO DO:

1. Protect the child from falling to the floor.

2. Roll the child to the side.

3. Clear the mouth of any vomit or saliva so he can breathe.

4. Don't try to place anything between the teeth.

5. Sponge the child with cool water. DON'T use ice, just cool tap water.

6. After the convulsion, NOTIFY THE PARENTS IMMEDIATELY. If the child remains unconscious, CALL 911.

7. Once the child is fully awake, give sips of water or juice. Just be sure he doesn't gag or choke on anything.

OBSTRUCTED AIRWAY

(CONSCIOUS INFANT, up to 12 months)

If the baby is actively coughing, do nothing. The object will probably release by itself. If no sound is heard, this is more serious.

WHAT TO DO:

1. Turn the baby's head down, and support him on an inner arm.

2. Place your thumb and index finger on his jaw. Be careful not to close off the Adam's apple,

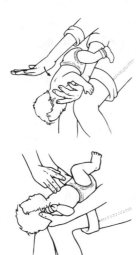

which will cut off the baby's air.

3. Give five firm blows between the baby's shoulder blades with the heel of your free hand. (See diagram.)

4. Turn the baby on his back with his head tilted down, facing you. Put one hand underneath, on his back.

5. Put two fingers (ring and middle) on the baby's chest, and give five quick thrusts, pressing down 1/2 to 1 inch. (See diagram.)

6. Turn the baby head down again. Keep repeating steps 1–5 until the foreign object is out—or the infant becomes unconscious.

OBSTRUCTED AIRWAY
(UNCONSCIOUS INFANT, up to 12 months)

WHAT TO DO:

1. Call out for help or call 911. Get a sibling to bring the phone to you, or pick up the baby and

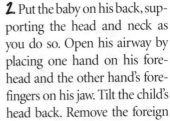

carry him to the phone.

2. Put the baby on his back, supporting the head and neck as you do so. Open his airway by placing one hand on his forehead and the other hand's forefingers on his jaw. Tilt the child's head back. Remove the foreign object only if you can see it.

3. Attempt to give rescue breaths by tilting the baby's head back slightly and then breathing over his mouth and nose, forming a tight seal.

4. If unsuccessful with rescue breaths, give the baby five blows on his back.

5. Turn the infant in a sandwich position as described above; give five chest thrusts.

6. Perform another tongue-jaw lift. Remove the foreign object only if you can see it.

7. Try again to give five rescue breaths.

8. Repeat these steps until you're successful, or until help arrives.

OBSTRUCTED AIRWAY

(CONSCIOUS CHILD, ages one to eight)

If the child is actively coughing or able to talk, do nothing. The object will probably release by itself. If no sound is heard, this is more serious.

WHAT TO DO:

> **NOTE:** *The Heimlich maneuver is an important life-saving technique. Although this section describes the technique, it is not intended as a substitute for formal training. You should obtain formal first-aid training that includes the performance of this maneuver.*

Perform abdominal thrusts. Stand behind the child, and wrap your arms around his waist. Make one hand into a fist, rest it slightly above the belly button, grasp the fist with the other

hand, and thrust upward into the child's stomach (Heimlich maneuver). Repeat until the foreign object is out—or the child becomes unconscious.

OBSTRUCTED AIRWAY
(UNCONSCIOUS CHILD, ages one to eight)

WHAT TO DO:

1. Call out for help or call 911.

2. Put the child on his back, supporting the head and neck as you do so. Open his airway by placing one hand on his forehead and the other hand's forefingers on his jaw. Tilt the child's head back. (See diagram on page 107.) Remove the foreign object only if you can see it.

3. Attempt to give rescue breaths by pinching the child's nose shut with your fingers, placing your mouth over the child's, and giving two quick breaths.

4. If unsuccessful, perform five abdominal thrusts, straddling the child's hips. Place the heel of one hand on the child's abdomen, slightly above the navel. Place your other hand on top of the first hand. Press both hands into the abdomen with a quick upward motion.

5. If you see the foreign object, remove it. If you don't see the object, go back to rescue breathing. If the airway remains obstructed (the chest does not rise), reposition the head and keep trying.

6. If the airway still remains obstructed, keep alternating with abdominal thrusts until you're successful, or until help arrives.

POISONING

You could have sworn that Joshua was upstairs in his room. You sent him up there to get his favorite book, but he's taken longer than usual. He bounds into the room with a big smile on his face, clutching his book in one hand, but you notice something in the other. He holds it up and says with the cutest smile, "I ate all the candy!" It's an empty baby Tylenol bottle.

Stop everything! This is serious business. When in doubt, assume the worst. Never think, *Oh, there is NO WAY this child could have swallowed this furniture polish!* He very well could have. Approximately 80 percent of

childhood poisonings occur between the ages of one and four. All drugs and household cleaning supplies should be locked away from children. This means even the simplest baby pain relievers.

Explain your upcoming actions to the child. Try not to appear too upset, but let him know he may have hurt himself.

WHAT TO DO:
1. Give the child a glass of milk immediately.
2. Most labels of household cleaning supplies carry warnings and treatment suggestions. Read the labels first.
3. Call the Poison Control Center or a hospital (ask for the emergency room). Find out what the specific treatment would be for whatever was swallowed, and follow the instructions closely.

HOW TO INDUCE VOMITING (if told to do so by the physician or Poison Control Center):
- Give syrup of ipecac if there is some in the house.
- Try placing a finger at the back of the child's throat to get him to gag.
- When the child does vomit, try to place the head lower than the chest, to prevent the vomit from entering the lungs.
- If you can't get the child to vomit, you must get him to a hospital as soon as possible.

HOWEVER, do not have the child vomit if he is:
- Convulsing.
- Unconscious.

- Has a burning sensation in his mouth or throat.
- Swallowed a corrosive agent such as dishwasher detergent, lye, bleach, disinfectant, drain opener, floor wax, kerosene, or grease remover or dissolver.

Call the parents immediately.

SHOCK

Shock can occur when there has been an injury to the body, even a minor one. Once in a while, the body is so jolted by an injury that it loses control of the circulatory system. This can happen even if there has been no injury at all. For example, if a person receives bad news, it can cause him to go into shock.

Look for the symptoms of shock. The skin is cold and clammy; the pulse is fast and weak; the face is pale. The child may complain of dizziness or nausea. Speech may be slurred. Restlessness and anxiety can ride along with the other symptoms.

WHAT TO DO:

1. Have the child lie down.

2. Elevate the legs two inches or more off the ground.

3. If there are injuries, handle the child carefully.
4. Keep the child warm but not hot. Use a blanket or a sheet, depending on the weather.
5. Call 911 and the parents immediately.

SPLINTERS

A small splinter projecting from the skin can usually be removed by a small tug using tweezers. If you can't remove it with tweezers, cover it with a Band-Aid and let the child know this is important and his parents will take care of it.

SPRAINS AND STRAINS

Little Bridget slipped off the swing and landed wrong. She can barely put weight on her foot, and it does seem a little swollen.

WHAT TO DO:
1. Carry the child into the house.
2. Place her on the sofa.
3. Elevate the injured area with a pillow.
4. Apply ice wrapped in a cloth to reduce pain and swelling.

5. Have the child rest quietly. This is a good time to play cards or read a good book, and wait for Mom or Dad.

STOMACH ACHES

If a child tells you his stomach hurts, ask specifically where it hurts. Many times children say that they have tummy aches because they don't want to do something, or they don't want to be alone. Sometimes a child can get angry and upset and cause himself a tummy ache! If the parents have left without mentioning that little Gabe has been complaining of stomach aches, it would be wise to think about what may have led to this announcement.

However, there is also the honest-to-goodness stomach ache.

WHAT TO DO:

Call the parents. They may tell you to give the child a spoonful of medicine or some other remedy. They may also decide to come home. It's their decision.

VOMITING

Usually, with children, this experience never gets any forewarning. Suddenly, the living room carpet or the couch is covered with . . . Ugh! The first thing you do is comfort the child and clean him up. Then keep him resting on the sofa or a chair while you clean up the mess. Use paper towels and sponges. Wet a towel and scrub the carpet or sofa till most of the stain is gone.

Keep a bucket or bowl handy to the child, with instructions

on why it's important to aim for the container next time. Notify parents, and open a window! Your little charge may tell you he is fine now and wants to eat. If age appropriate, give him an ice cube to suck on instead. If the child is very young, let him have a few sips of water. We recommend avoiding even liquids, however, because, as a rule, everything comes back up.

HOUSEHOLD EMERGENCIES

ELECTRICAL FAILURE

First, look outside. Is the whole neighborhood dark, or just your house?

If it's just your house, check the main circuit breaker box for a thrown switch (you asked the parents about the box location at the beginning of the evening, remember?). Return any "Off" switch to "On," and you're back in business.

If it goes off again, you have an overloaded circuit of some kind (too many electrical demands all at once, such as an iron + a hair dryer + a curling iron + ?????). Turn some of the appliances off, and then reset the switch.

If the problem can't be resolved, or the whole neighborhood is dark, get out the flashlight and make a game of it. If you don't have a flashlight, find some candles. Use holders to place them securely, and keep them up, out of the reach of little fingers.

Usually, when the electricity is off, the phone still works. Call the electric company and give them the address of where you are. *(Remember, you asked for this information when you first arrived at the house.)*

There is no reason to leave the house. Sing songs with the kids, or tell nice stories that don't scare them.

FIRE

Your only concern is to get the children out and safely across the street or to a neighbor's. Then call 911. Do not go back into a burning house, no matter what you left behind (your purse, your homework, etc.).

GAS LEAK

Open a window. Then immediately get the children out of the house. Take them to a neighbor you trust, or go across the street away from the house. Locate a phone to call the gas company or 911. Then call the parents.

OBSCENE PHONE CALLS

Never get caught up in a conversation with these types. Simply hang up. If someone calls again, hang up. If they continue to call, take the phone off the hook.

If the house where you are sitting has an answering machine, let the machine pick up the call. That way, you know who is calling, and you can decide whether to respond. Nothing is more exciting for this type of lowlife than to engage a person in conversation. Don't give him the satisfaction.

PROWLER

Call 911 immediately IF you really saw someone.

If you only think you heard something, do not go out and investigate. Call the parents and tell them. If you can't reach them, call your parents. Lock all doors and windows.

If you actually see someone, try to remember his clothing and his approximate height. Any description is helpful and will enable the police to be on the lookout. If you see him walk away, tell the police in what direction he went. If you see him get into a car, try to remember what the car looked like. To be a real hero, get the license number. *(But don't risk going outside.)*

NATURAL DISASTERS

EARTHQUAKE

Surprise! It happens when you least expect it. Since you are the boss, you keep your cool. If you are calm, the kids will be also.

If you're indoors:

1. Get under a table (unless it has a glass top), a desk, or a bed. Or brace yourself and the kids under a strong doorway.

2. Keep children away from falling objects. Watch for books tumbling off shelves, or ceramics crashing down from mantels.

3. Stay away from windows and mirrors.

If you're outdoors:

1. Move kids to an open area away from houses, apartments, tall buildings, walls, power lines, power poles, trees, brick walls, or any other object that could fall.

2. Lie down flat in the open.

After the shaking has stopped, put on your best smile and say something like "Wow, that was really something, huh? Like a roller-coaster ride! Have you ever felt an earthquake before?" Let the children tell you how they feel.

Check for broken glass whether you're inside or out. Put shoes and socks on little feet to avoid cuts. Use your first-aid kit if needed.

Check for gas leaks. If you can figure out how to turn off the gas, do it. If you smell gas, get out of the house. Take the kids across the street or to a reliable neighbor. DON'T turn lights on or off. DON'T light matches or do anything that makes a spark.

Run some water from the tap into the tub or a container. If you suspect line damage, then turn the water off at the main valve.

If it was a bad quake, turn off the main power switch, because once the electric company restores power, a flood of electricity into the house could cause an electrical short, which in turn could spark and ignite the gas. It's probably best to unplug all electrical items: clocks, appliances, radios, televisions, etc.

If it wasn't a bad quake, turn on the TV or radio for advisories. Be prepared for aftershocks, and prepare your little ones, too. No doubt the parents will be calling to check on you and their kids. If phone lines are out, stay calm. Turn on the TV and listen to newscasters; they generally have much excellent information.

Confine family pets.

If you are trapped, shout or whistle. If help is a long time coming, knock three times on a regular basis, and wait and listen. Continue the pattern of knocks until you know someone has heard you.

If it's dark and you can't see, explore with your knuckles, not fingers (due to broken glass), crawling along walls, feeling as you go.

Don't allow children to rub their eyes. Keep thumb-suckers' thumbs clean.

If police or fire/rescue officials evacuate you, leave a message for the parents on the door as to where you are being taken. Try to describe your intended route.

FLOOD

Usually, there is forewarning. Call for help, and get to higher ground with the children. If you can turn off the main electrical switch, do it.

If this is a flood from a toilet or under a kitchen sink, and not the mighty Mississippi, look for a knob attached to a pipe and turn it. If you can clean up the mess, great! Don't use the best towels in the house; look for rags or old towels. If something is totally beyond you, call the parents.

HURRICANE

You probably will have plenty of warning—which means you're unlikely to be baby-sitting in these conditions! But if you are, stay on the highest possible ground. Cooperate with officials who come to your door, and don't forget to leave a note in the house, informing the parents that you've been evacuated to a shelter.

TORNADO

For a "Tornado Watch," bring family pets indoors, gather the children, and stay tuned to the TV for further information.

During a "Tornado Warning" (which means an actual tornado has been spotted nearby), move everybody immediately to the basement or a storm cellar. If there is no cellar or basement, lie flat under a table or under the stairway. Don't place the children, yourself, or pets near any windows.

If you are outdoors, lie down flat in a low place like a ditch.

Conclusion

THE MAGIC KEY WITH CHILDREN: ENCOURAGEMENT

I (Mary) will never forget the time years ago when I was sitting by a friend watching our year-old babies have swim lessons. There was my precious Joshua, buoyed up only by a wet suit, bobbing up and down as his instructor taught him how to save himself. I sat there holding my breath, hiding behind my fingers, feeling my heart pounding, and dreading everything my poor baby was going through.

Then it was Henson's turn. My friend Donna jumped up, ran to the edge of the pool, and shouted at her son, "You can do it, Henson! That's great! Try it again! Good job!" I sat there changing Josh and watching her encourage and bolster her son through the entire lesson. I was so impressed! Henson smiled and cooed at the instructor, beamed at his mother, and was in no way stressed.

I started taking lessons from Donna that day. I really liked what I heard and the results it got.

Another time, my sister Therese and I were watching our children play in the backyard. Suddenly, our conversation was interrupted by loud complaints and hot tears. "Bridget called me a name!"

All parties involved were called over to our table, where Therese said, "Look at your sister. Do you see the result of calling her that name? It hurt her feelings. Please apologize and remember that this is a safe house where feelings are important. We don't call each other names, or tease or insult one another."

A couple of weeks later when I heard a visiting child use bad language, the children themselves stopped playing and told the child that that kind of talk was not allowed in their "safe" home. The kid looked a little stunned but went along with the house rules. What a lesson he learned that day! Can you imagine him going home to his parents at dinner and asking if their home could be safe also?

Children do not naturally know all the right things to do and say, but they are wonderfully trainable. Here is a list of encouragements we use and have heard used by friends. Some of them I have posted on my refrigerator, so when I'm right in the middle of dinner preparations and Josh comes in with a problem or is unhappy, I just glance at my list and choose an encouragement that works!

50 WAYS TO ENCOURAGE CHILDREN

1. You can do it!
2. Awesome!
3. Way to go!
4. Good job!
5. I knew you could do it!
6. Outstanding!
7. You're so special.
8. Nice work.
9. You're really growing up.

10. I love you.

11. I love your manners!

12. You're amazing!

13. You mean the world to me.

14. You're a winner!

15. You sure are getting responsible!

16. I trust you.

17. You're catching on!

18. You make me so happy!

19. Excellent work!

20. You're very responsible.

21. You're important!

22. You brighten my day!

23. What a trouper!

24. Thank you!

25. You're a team player!

26. You're wonderful!

27. I'm proud of you.

28. I like your attitude!

29. I like the way you're trying!

30. You've improved!

31. You're getting better.

32. Things are looking up!

33. You're a great help!

34. I like the way you did that.

35. You make me smile.

36. You're special just the way you are.

37. That's a wonderful quality you have.

38. Thank you for being honest.

39. You're a kind brother/sister.

40. You help make this a safe house.

41. "Terrific" must be your middle name.

42. Do you have any idea just how wonderful you are?

43. That was very wise of you.

44. Have I told you lately how much I love you?

45. I appreciate the way you're listening.

46. You make baby-sitting fun!

47. You're a blessing to me!

48. Thank you for asking.

49. I like the way you treat others.

50. That took a lot of courage!

For Your Eyes—And Ears—Only!

Resources From Focus on the Family®

Brio Magazine

YES, there's a magazine that's written and designed for you, today's Christian teenage girl, and *Brio* is it! Each issue is filled with interesting articles, great stories, faith-boosting devotions, music reviews, and advice on everything from fashion and food to having fun with friends and getting to know the opposite sex—all from a biblical perspective! What could be better? Read it every month!

"The Christy Miller Series"

Teens all across the nation have made this series from Robin Jones Gunn a best seller! Now you can find out for yourself why the series is so popular as you become friends with Christy Miller—a teen who makes a commitment to Christ in the first book and then grows in her walk with the Lord in the next 11 paperbacks. Don't miss a single one!

Tune in to *Life on the Edge—LIVE!*

Sure, your parents give the best advice. But when you want an *unbiased* opinion—or simply want to hear what other teens are dealing with—tune in to *Life on the Edge—LIVE!* Hosted by Dr. Joe White and Susie Shellenberger, this nationally syndicated live call-in radio show gives you a safe place to talk about what's on your mind.

For more information or to request any of these resources, simply write to Focus on the Family, Colorado Springs, CO 80995, or call 1-800-A-FAMILY (1-800-232-6459). Friends in Canada may write Focus on the Family, P.O. Box 9800, Stn. Terminal, Vancouver, B.C. V6B 4G3, or call 1-800-661-9800.

Visit our Web site—www.family.org—to learn more about the ministry or to find out if there is a Focus on the Family office in your country.

FOCUS ON THE FAMILY®

Welcome to the Family!

Whether you received this book as a gift, borrowed it from
a friend, or purchased it yourself, we're glad you read it!
It's just one of the many helpful, insightful and encouraging
resources produced by Focus on the Family.

In fact, that's what Focus on the Family is all about—
providing inspiration, information and biblically based
advice to people in all stages of life.

It began in 1977 with the vision of one man, Dr. James Dobson,
a licensed psychologist and author of 16 best-selling books on
marriage, parenting, and family. Alarmed by the societal, political,
and economic pressures that were threatening the existence
of the American family, Dr. Dobson founded Focus on the Family
with one employee—an assistant—and a once-a-week
radio broadcast, aired on only 36 stations.

Now an international organization, Focus on the Family is
dedicated to preserving Judeo-Christian values and strengthening
the family through more than 70 different ministries, including
eight separate daily radio broadcasts; television public service
announcements; 11 publications; and a steady series of books
and award-winning films and videos for people
of all ages and interests.

Recognizing the needs of, as well as the sacrifices and important
contribution made by, such diverse groups as educators, physi-
cians, attorneys, crisis pregnancy center staff and single parents,
Focus on the Family offers specific outreaches to uphold and min-
ister to these individuals, too. And it's all done for one purpose,
and one purpose only: to encourage and strengthen individuals
and families through the life-changing message of Jesus Christ.

• • •

For more information about the ministry, or if we can be of help to
your family, simply write to Focus on the Family, Colorado Springs,
CO 80995 or call 1-800-A-FAMILY (1-800-232-6459). Friends in
Canada may write Focus on the Family, P.O. Box 9800, Stn.
Terminal, Vancouver, B.C. V6B 4G3 or call 1-800-661-9800.

Visit our Web site—www.family.org—to learn more about the ministry
or to find out if there is a Focus on the Family office in your country.

We'd love to hear from you!